The Little Peul

CARAF Books

Caribbean and African Literature Translated from French

Carrol F. Coates, Editor

Clarisse Zimra, J. Michael Dash,
and Elisabeth Mudimbe-Boyi,
Advisory Editors

Mariama Barry

The Little Peul

Translated by Carrol F. Coates

Afterword by Irène Assiba d'Almeida

University of Virginia Press
Charlottesville and London

Ouvrage publié avec le soutien du Centre national du livre—ministère français chargé de la culture.

Publication of this translation was assisted by a grant from the French Ministry of Culture, National Center of the Book.

Originally published in French as *La Petite Peule,* © Librairie Arthème Fayard, 2000

University of Virginia Press
Translation and afterword © 2010
by the Rector and Visitors of the University of Virginia

LIBRARY OF CONGRESS CATALOGING-IN-PUBLICATION DATA

Barry, Mariama.
  [Petite Peule. English]
  The little Peul / Mariama Barry ; translated by Carrol F. Coates ; afterword by Irène Assiba d'Almeida.
     p.   cm. — (CARAF books)
  ISBN 978-0-8139-2962-0 (acid-free paper) — ISBN 978-0-8139-2963-7 (pbk. : acid-free paper) — 978-0-8139-2968-2
  I. Coates, Carrol F., 1930– II. Title.
  PQ3989.2.B335P4813 2010
  843'.92—dc22   2009036543

CONTENTS

A NOTE FROM THE TRANSLATOR

Dear Little Peul,

Here is the promised English version of *The Little Peul*. The translator has done his job, for better or for worse.

Readers of the translation may not be highly interested in the process of translation, and yet I have an inner compulsion to say that this English text is the result of a very personal and perhaps improbable reaction. Your story and your manner of writing it resonated within me . . . even if I never experienced the exact hardships and family problems with which you grew up.

I know that Little Peul, the narrator, often coincides with the author, Mariama Barry. I think, however, that Mariama intends this narrative to highlight the difficult existence of young girls and adolescents with a strong will to move beyond rigid traditional social and religious constraints for women and to affirm their own individuality.

It was a challenge for me to try to convey your intense personal tone through my English rendering. Although I have never had the opportunity to visit Dakar or the Fuuta Jaloo, I have in my mind strolled through the neighborhoods where you lived in Dakar, smelling the *ceebu jén* and turning my head away from the odiferous *yéet*. I have hiked the mountains around Kouye, and I can still see the grass ceiling inside Paty's house, smoke-blackened from the perpetual little fire.

As much as time allowed, I have familiarized myself with Wolof and Pulaar lexicons in order to "hear" the words you recall from your youth—*jaaraama*! I can only hope that you will not resent the fact that I have done my best to convert your gallicized orthography (justified for your French readers) to a "standard" orthography for each language.

You have told an intimate story to powerful effect. I will be

A NOTE FROM THE TRANSLATOR

pleased if anglophone readers are captivated by a lively sense of the realities you recount and by deep indignation at the atrocities committed by certain president-dictators whose names we would prefer not to honor in print (and the first president of Guinea was foremost among them for you).

I remain your respectful servant . . .

The translator

P.S. It is fitting that I thank several friends, students, and associates for their assistance. Three persons gave a careful reading of the manuscript—Professors Marilyn Gaddis Rose and Irène Assiba d'Almeida, along with Rachel Ginsberg (a former student). I am indebted to Juliana Makuchi Nfah-Abbenyi, Amy Baram Reid, and Lisa Tagliaferri for several forms of valuable help. Insightful linguistic and cultural consultation was given by several African colleagues—Moussa Kane, Cheikh Thiam, Jean Ouedraogo, and Karim Traoré.

The Little Peul

To Paty, Hadjiratou Barry

A vague uneasiness had come over me for several days without my knowing why. I could have figured out a true threat by hidden signs, the way you stalk small game on the savannah. I was powerless when it happened. Even yesterday, I was happy just listening to the sound of the beads strung around my skinny waist. My beads were in the shape of multi-colored lozenges and crescents threaded on several strands. I also had a number of charms—some slashes and crosses (to protect me against the evil eye . . . and gossip); I was wearing a copper ankle bracelet instead of the tiny bells I had worn when I was little to keep my mother aware of my whereabouts. I was wearing *dibe.**

All these objects weighed quite a bit. I didn't even know how long I had been wearing them. Forever!

Mama was embroidering some other charms on a piece of white cloth to wear around my neck.

"We're going to Fann to stay with your uncle. I'm going to take off all those charms you're wearing now."

For the first time in my life, I found myself without a single string on me, and I had the impression of being completely naked. What kind of bizarre ceremony was I headed for without my beads?

Under any other circumstances, I would have done anything to go to Fann! There were playing fields and toboggans there. I loved to go—it was a way to get out of our ghetto. But now, I was naked and light as a leaf that might be blown away at any instant by a whirlwind.

*Earrings made of gold that Peul mothers place on their daughters' ears. [All notes are by Mariama Barry unless otherwise specified.— *Trans.*]

"We'll go to the dressmaker's first to get your outfit."
The outfit was a pagne and a little red boubou* printed with drawings of ducks.
"You'll find some other girls there . . ."
Mama began to list the names of girls who were not my usual playmates. The only things these unknown girls and I had in common were the customs our parents persisted in making us follow by all possible means.

We were *ndjudu*,† part of the first or second generation of Peul parents from Guinea. We used to see each other when we attended Peul festivities with our families, but not very often. My own playmates were the ones I played with all the time around home—we shared everything, including punishment.

I had been kept away from them all day. I even had the right to do nothing. I had been forbidden to go play. Strange! The sound of their games didn't reach me. Had they been playing? I would never know.

I kept asking my mother why we didn't leave. Mama knew I was impatient as soon as there was any talk of travel or play.

"Your friends will be here before long," she repeated.

I heard the call of the muezzin for the final evening prayer, and I was beginning to wonder. Papa had not come home; he was with my brother, Laye. Even when he was late, Papa usually came back to sleep. I would have liked for him to be there. He would touch our chests in a habitual gesture, as if he wanted to make sure we were still alive. Since I was very little, I had always played a game by not lying down in my usual place and pretending to be asleep. Then, my father would come pick me up and carry me back to my own sleeping place. I would wrap my arms around him and burst out laughing. He always answered, "You won again!"

*A simple robe. [Originally, a Malinke word for the pelt of a monkey.—*Trans.*]
†Children born in Senegal of Peul parents from Guinea. [*Ndjudu dieri* are Peul born outside the village; *ndjudu walo* are those born within the village.—*Trans.*]

Only then could I go to sleep.

Instead of the routine, my mother was standing guard, without making it obvious, as if she thought I might escape. She gave me a ritual bath, made me drink some holy water, and massaged me with the rest of it. She put the white gris-gris around my neck.

Someone had just knocked at our door. A stout, middle-aged woman (about forty-five years old) came in—a person who was always at our feasts, and I didn't like her. She was followed by a group of eleven girls—the ones we were expecting. They too had white charms around their necks and were wearing new clothes. We looked at each other without speaking; like me, they didn't seem to know why we were there. The woman had us stretch out on mats. This didn't look good. I remembered then what Mama had said about this woman.

"She is one of our slaves; she is the keeper of our traditions; she will go with you from birth, through the excision, to your marriage."

I had no idea what all this mystery was about.

Very early the next morning, seeming even more authoritarian than the evening before, this woman was the first one on her feet. She shook all of us. We were assembled in record time.

All twelve of us headed for what I had heard called the *abattoir.**

In the group, there was even the daughter of the keeper of our traditions. She was older than us by far. She was twelve years old and had budding little breasts. The rest of us were in the six- to seven-year-old group. They began with her. In the back of the courtyard, we heard a quick, muffled cry. Then I realized what was coming. I got up and dashed out: I wanted to go home. But I was caught. First one, then another one of the women present took hold of me while I fought like a de-

*Slaughter house [French]. There is a possible double entendre: "Abattoirs" is a section of Dakar neighboring Rebeus, where Papa had a store.—*Trans.*

mon. I was thrown down on the mat. The fat woman sat on my child's breast and held my legs spread out. It did no good to bite her behind—I couldn't yell any more. I couldn't breathe with all her weight on me. I could sense the contact of a cutting tool between my legs. At that instant, I did not feel the pain, and I didn't see the butcher's weapon or her face. She immediately carried me into another room, where a mat, and her own daughter's cry of pain, awaited me. She stopped us short.

"Whatever you do, don't cry. If you cry, you'll cry the rest of your life."

And she left at once to deal with another victim who would undergo the same fate. My legs were numb, but, in a few minutes, a terrible pain, a wild pain that I can never describe took hold of me.

I didn't even notice that the woman had just placed the next little girl, who seemed to have fainted, beside me on the mat. The same order rang out.

"Don't cry! You have to stay with your legs straight and held apart, and don't lie on your side until you have completely healed!"

After all twelve girls had gone through this trial, the room where we were began to fill with *griottes*.* They kept dancing and chanting praises of each family and about our "bravery." Our mothers came in afterward with other women relatives and friends. They gave money to the chanters, but I would rather have made them shut up.

Our butcher was all smiles. The families congratulated her. Then they congratulated the huge woman who had brought us there. She pointed at us.

"These girls are to be congratulated also—they did not cry once during the experience. Not a single cry."

She must have been making fun of us, unless this was her way of encouraging us. I didn't want to think about my misfor-

---

*A woman of the *griot* caste, a type of traditional African singer.

tune. The more I thought about it, the less I could bear what I had undergone and the world around me. I had a hard time holding back my furious desire to throw all these women out and to scream with all my might.

At that point, I really had to stifle the insane desire to yell. I would have liked to let all that out, in the depth of some forest, with a heartrending cry that would wake all the creatures living there. Then I would faint so I wouldn't see them gobble me up.

I was expecting to see my father; with him, I could cry my heart out. I asked Mama if he was going to come.

"Stop crying and behave like a big girl," she answered. "Don't look too hard for your father to come. The world you have just entered is a world of women. No man is ever allowed to enter it."

I stopped listening to my mother and, still lying there, I let myself go and was content to squeeze the hands of those good women who came to "congratulate" us. They asked us how we were, as if we were ill, and gave us money as presents.

When the visitors left, we didn't talk much to one another. I kept losing blood and refused to eat.

On the evening of the second day, my father finally came to see me. As soon as I saw him, I wanted to run meet him as usual. But I was so weak I could only whimper and repeat, "Papa came! Papa came to see me."

The tears I had held back kept streaming and blurred my vision. I was sure he had come to take me back home. Mama had taken advantage of his absence to hurt me, just as she did when she used to punish me, and I would wait for Papa's return to start crying again so he would console me as he asked, "What did you do?"

But this time, I hadn't done anything. And they had hurt me badly.

Papa was so distant that I would have preferred for him not to come. He spoke to me as if I were a stranger. I wanted to yell that it was really me in case he had not recognized me. It seemed that the experience I had just undergone had made my childhood disappear. I no longer had a right to the tenderness he had let me grow accustomed to—it was apparently reserved for the very young.

Exactly like Mama, he told me, "You know, now you are a big girl . . ."

With these words, we separated. That was the only time he came to see me. I began crying again, convinced that the order not to cry related only to physical pain and that I was free to complain about my unhappiness. Wrong! As soon as my father walked away, the butcher told me, in no uncertain terms, to dry my tears. She ordered food brought to me.

"You are going to eat like a big girl or else I will feed you by force, stuff it down your throat like a goose. Your father was only here because someone told him you were refusing to eat and were losing blood."

Because she stood facing me, I closed my eyes (this was only the beginning) so I wouldn't see her or what I was eating. My tears kept coming. She finally pulled the bowl away and spoke again.

"You will start eating one of these days. A month is a short time to fast . . ."

Every two days, she treated us with Mercurochrome that she applied with a bit of cotton. As a matter of economy, the same piece of cotton was used to treat all the girls.

"Don't cry . . . you have to hold in your complaints and take control of your body."

The only solution was to weep in silence.

I had the impression that time was passing slowly. We helped with housework—peeling vegetables, washing dishes, etc.—without ever going outside. We could have visits only during the afternoon. Our mothers came and talked among themselves. Laye had followed my mother to see me. The woman who had mutilated me simply chased him away. Mama pleaded with her.

"He's only a child, not yet four years old."

"He's still a boy!"

Mama cut her visit short to go home with my little brother, who must have been missing me. My mother had only the two of us.

We had been there almost a month. One day passed like the others without my becoming more communicative. And when she applied medication one day, the woman told us, "You have healed, and I'm going to check with your families about the day you should leave."

No doubt, it would be a day when the cycle of the moon was right, and offerings would be made in order to protect us and keep away any evil spirits.

When the day came, late one evening, the fat woman who had accompanied us a month earlier was there. She had brought new clothes obtained from our parents. For the first time, we had the right to a full bath. We went to bed early since we had to be ready at the same time as the day she had led us away at the muezzin's first call. And before daybreak, each girl would be taken to her family on foot.

I couldn't sleep. I was going to leave those companions—the ones with whom I had suffered, undergone the same torture, and received the same nourishment. But I was impatient to get home and see my friends again.

Mama was there, but not my father or brother, just as it had been on the eve of my sacrifice.

Mama tried to reassure me that the woman had done her duty well. I had to spread my thighs again and undergo the inquisitorial finger. She seemed to be satisfied. After washing me and giving me holy water to drink, she told me to close my eyes. I heard her recite some words and then she put my *dibe* back on.

"You know that you belong to a very hierarchical society— there are trials you have to undergo at each stage in order to go from one level to the next. I might even say from one world to another."

It was as if these memories had some charm for her.

"The week you were born, I pierced your ears with a needle and thread so they would not become infected. I applied several drops of my milk and twisted the thread before putting the *dibe* on. That was your first initiation. The second was placing you in the coranic school so you could turn toward your Creator, learn to do your ablutions, your prayers, and recite the Qur'an properly. As for what just took place, it has made you grow because you had not yet experienced suffering. You were a child who knew only joy and had no cares. Because this trial was painful, it has brought you a new power, that of overcoming suffering. And when you are older, your menstruation will begin. That will give you access to the world of women. On your wedding night, as soon as your husband has taken your virginity, you will be an adult woman. And as a woman, when you have your first child, you will crouch with your teeth biting into a rag or a piece of wood, because you must not cry out. And, with your first child, you will finally be like me. You will have experienced all that I have experienced, and in the same order."

She added: "That's why, when the French military doctor helped with my delivery and told me, 'You have a daughter, it's a daughter,' I was happy. And at the same time, I felt sorry for you because I knew what awaited you."

Then she went on, "I can still see myself—I must have been seventeen years old when I became pregnant. That same doctor had just told me the news. I returned to your father and told him I wanted to go back to my parents. Your father persuaded me not to leave. He found it normal that a married woman was expecting."

Something else interested me now.

"Mama, why didn't I go through this trial with my friends, Kumba, Kine, and Sara?"

"They will never have that experience. You are a bit different through the customs of your ancestors. It's nothing serious for you—you're still intact with just a little 'wound' that you received in keeping with the tradition. You'll forget it quickly.

You might have belonged to a group of people whose traditions require a supplementary trial."

I learned that, for the "supplementary trial," the vaginal opening is reduced to a minimum and that, on the wedding night, the proud husband expects to deflower his wife and to penetrate her "fortress" in spite of her cries of pain. If he doesn't succeed, the butcher, supposed to have disappeared forever, will reappear. She will then take charge of enlarging the orifice with a sharp object in order to let the husband fulfill his role.

"We women always have to undergo trials; and we are the guardians of tradition for our female offspring, even when blood has to flow . . ."

I listened to my mother in silence. This was our first conversation. I didn't ask any more questions.

I was very calm. The arrival of my father and brother kept us from continuing our women's talk. But maybe she didn't have anything else to tell me.

I had noticed that my father was away only at important moments. That couldn't be the result of pure chance.

I was waiting for daybreak to see my friends. I was tired, but I didn't want to go to bed. As soon as I left our room, I went to the room of my friend, Kumba, who went to tell the others I was back.

I had become a curiosity, and they assailed me with questions.

"Why did they do that to you and not to us?"

"Does it hurt?"

"Yes."

"What did they do to you?"

How should I answer those questions? I couldn't tell them what had happened, not even the reason for it. As to what they had done to me, I wasn't too sure since, before this trial, I had never paid any particular attention to this intimate part of my body. I knew it was there when I felt the need to pee. I was conscious of the stream that I could stop whenever I wished.

"Mama told me that we are different, that you will never experience what happened to me."

"So, show us, we want to see."

"No."

I was afraid that they would touch me and hurt me since the slightest touch on that part of my body made me groan.

The difference that was beginning to grow between us would keep me apart from them for a while. We needed some time for things to get back to where they were before, more or less. Finally, the questions stopped. We began to wash together to scrub each other's backs the way we did before. But Mama's words kept resonating in my head for a long time. She had probably just repeated what she herself had heard from her mother, and the latter from her mother before.

I already knew that I would not pass on this traumatizing experience. And, in fact, I was to fight much later to be the only sacrificial victim within and beyond my family.

There were five of us: my parents, my brother Laye, who is two years younger, and a servant who came to help with the housework every day. My father had a shop near a camp where married military personnel lived, along the corniche in Dakar. All the military personnel of French West Africa, the Senegalese riflemen, were based at this camp. This is where I saw the light of day. It was a bustling neighborhood. People of various countries and origins lived there side by side.

Every morning, Papa played sports with the soldiers, and in the evening, his shop was the meeting point where this fine society came together. Like a good businessman, he could get along in all their languages.

I had *Portocaisse** neighbors who would go to get feed for their hogs in the great communal vats. This was the period when local people, apparently to show off their opulence, used to prepare huge quantities of *ceeb,*† dripping with oil, throwing the leftovers in the public dump, to the great delight of pig owners.

I liked to go over to the neighbors, who had a daughter my age. Whenever I came back, Mama would sniff my mouth and ask whether I had eaten there. As if sniffing me weren't enough, she washed me and changed my clothes right away.

"You smell like a pigpen!"

I didn't dare tell her that my girlfriend and I rode the pigs. The condition of my dress and the stench were enough to give me away. But the idea that I might have gotten close to the

---

*Persons from Cape Verde, a former Portuguese colony.
†Rice and fish, a national dish of Senegal. [*Ceeb* is the word for rice; *ceebu jén* is the full expression for rice with fish.—*Trans.*]

beasts and, even worse, might have ridden them would have been unbearable for my mother.

My teeth were cleaned with laundry detergent into which Mama dipped my toothbrush. Afterward came the toothpick and Mama's index finger, before rinsing. My brother made fun of me, but he got the same treatment. Our mouths were on fire, worse than from hot peppers. Then she would lecture us.

"Don't forget that nobody will listen to a person with bad breath."

Our baby teeth survived this treatment like all the rest.

My mother, a Peul from the mountains of the Fuuta Jaloo in Guinea, did not like seafood. She went into a rage when my brother and I ate crabs. We were served in separate glasses and bowls, contrary to the custom of eating from a common bowl around which the family gathered.

Mama was allergic to those creepy crawly things. And, anyway, she could see filth everywhere. Without provocation, she would wash and change us several times a day. When she decided we were too dirty, she filled two large tubs with water, one for my brother, the other for me. We had to sit there, face to face, waiting for her to take care of us. She left us soaking like dirty laundry, and with a coarse sponge, she would vigorously scrub our entire bodies. When we were lucky, we were saved from this domestic drowning by the arrival of Papa, who would take us out of the bath. Mama would protest.

"Are you sure they're clean?"

"They're perfectly clean! Tell me how many baths you've put them through today?"

Mama would always say, without lifting her eyes from her knitting or embroidering, "This is their second bath."

Then my brother and I would secretly show him our fingers so he could see the approximate number.

Often, I had two baths more than my brother, who always managed to escape in time. I would be at my fifth bath when my father got home; that was the average with Mama.

As he dressed us, Papa would comment.

"With all the baths you've had, you can give up bathing when you're grown!"

My brother must have taken Papa at his word. The only showers he took later were from unexpected rainstorms.

The maid complained, when Mama wasn't listening. "I think it's strange that anyone would love water so much. Look at the clothes she wants me to wash—they've been washed and ironed. For her, 'wrinkled' means 'dirty,' and she sees 'micropes' everywhere. We won't say a thing, will we? I'm going to put them neatly back in place."

I liked the maid. She let me in on her misfortunes. In the evening, she took my brother and me for a walk on the corniche by the ocean. She would often manage to bring us back just at sunset so we could skip the last bath. After a certain time, Mama would just grumble and give us a quick washing.

We ate dinner relatively early, before the clients came to the store to begin talking.

Mama put us to bed immediately; she fell asleep before we did. Then my brother and I would get up and tiptoe to our father's side. We would stay with him until the last customer left. Papa would close the shop and put the money drawer on the floor. He would take out the rare bills; as for my brother and me, we each had a pile of coins that we arranged by size. Papa would recount them afterward. Then we went to bed, being careful not to awaken Mama.

Mornings, I was the only one to get *fonde** for breakfast, delivered by a tall, skinny woman. I loved it. She always came by with her calabash full of steaming porridge. She would be chewing on a toothpick that she removed for an instant just to give us a big smile that moved me. She was a well-liked vendor with a sizeable clientele. She went home once her calabash had been emptied. Her visit was the beginning of my day.

*Millet porridge.

I also had a friend who was dirty, usually half naked, a bit crazy, but not at all threatening. People said that he had buried a treasure somewhere but couldn't remember the place. Children threw rocks at him. That made me feel sorry for him. One day he disappeared. I missed him for quite a while. In desperation, I would wait for him at the place where he usually sat. Then Mama would take me back to the house and put me in the water to soak.

My parents got along well. Papa played with us a lot. When he wanted to remain alone with my mother, he sent us to see the marabout, a coal merchant who had his shop a few meters from Papa's store.

The marabout taught the Qur'an to young children, and I would visit him with my *alluwal*,* on which a line was inscribed. As a merchant, this man kept old newspapers that he placed in his clients' baskets, which often had holes in the bottom. Although I couldn't read, I liked to leaf through the newspapers, pretending to read.

*A wooden plank, used as a slate by little children in the coranic school.

Papa made kites for us from tree leaves. We had a lot of fun with them. We were the only kids who had them. One day, a tragedy almost happened: towing his kite with me following, my brother found himself between the wheels of a car. Miraculously, he came out of it without the slightest scratch. Mama was tremendously frightened and wouldn't stop crying and demanding that we move immediately, as far as possible from the road.

The evening of the accident, Mama served us but refused to eat with us. She was deeply shaken and only wanted to hug us tightly to her.

From that day on, we were to become her prisoners. Mama wouldn't let us go out any more with our father or the maid. Our only playground was beneath the bar in my father's shop. From then on, we were enveloped by the maternal presence everywhere we went, in all circumstances and at all places.

My brother and I took a malicious pleasure in asking to go to the toilet, each in turn. As soon as one would come back, the other would go, with our unfortunate mother trailing along. For us, this was a new game in which she participated as victim.

Papa would say, "The President of the Republic himself doesn't have his bodyguards with him twenty-four out of twenty-four hours . . ."

Under pressure from our mother, Papa gave in to a move. Unfortunately, everything he found still seemed to be too close to the hellish traffic. He finally found a house that suited the maternal requirements, but he forgot about the state of the property.

In our hurry, we took away only a few items on a cart drawn by a frighteningly skinny horse who seemed to beg for mercy.

The new house was located in La Médina on a very narrow little pedestrian street. The dwellings were squeezed close to one another. They were overpopulated shacks, judging from the number of people sitting outside. We had only one bedroom in one of the shacks, covered with red tiles beneath the fronds of a coconut tree. When it was windy, I was always afraid a coconut would fall on our heads.

Mama put my brother and me to bed on a mat, with a coarse blanket.

I wasn't at all interested in going to bed.

I was curious to discover and explore our new space.

The first evening, I asked Mama to go to the toilet with me, hoping she would let me go alone, allowing me to escape her watchful eye and explore the unknown surroundings. She asked a wife of the *borom-kër** where it was.

"I beg your pardon for not showing you the whole place—I was waiting for your husband to come back. You'll see that it doesn't take long: the enclosure you see in front of us is where we wives and our young children live; in the one on the left, there are the older children who don't live with us much anymore; and as for the enclosure where you live, there are only tenants and their children. I am the first wife—you're going to meet my two co-wives along with their children and mine . . . Oh! the toilets and the showers are public and they're not far from here—only about two hundred meters. They're well built and separated into two parts: the men's side and the women's side. Our property is surrounded by three public fountains—they are all at the same distance. The mayor of Dakar did a good job and we are grateful to him . . . We will always vote for him."

Then she poured forth a flood of praise for the mayor.

"Mama, *saw saw*,"† I repeated, feeling that I was neglected because of the enthusiasm of this lady, who was already calling Mama "my daughter."

Only then did the woman deign to look at me, as if she suddenly remembered the question Mama had asked her.

Mama was listening politely. I had let go of her hand and I relieved myself right there in the courtyard. When Mama started to scold me, the lady protested.

*The owner of the house.
†Peepee.

"She's only a child. Just throw a little water on it so it doesn't smell of pee."

Mama stopped smiling then. She interrupted the lady on the pretext that she had to put me to bed.

This time, she was holding me firmly by the hand.

Papa arrived that evening with the rest of the baggage. Mama spoke to him right away.

"Do you know that we don't have either a toilet or running water in this house?"

On the other hand, they did provide electricity, most likely for fear that candles or kerosene lamps would burn the neighborhood down.

"At least that's one thing to bring us a bit closer to civilization," said Papa.

Stubbornly, Mama answered: "This is serious—we have to move again. I can't stay in this house one more day!"

"At least give me time to organize our possessions."

Papa looked beaten.

"I'll start to look for another place to live, I promise."

That calmed Mama down, and she began to put our baggage in temporary order.

The sound of a wheezing Vélosolex* interrupted our games and hubbub. I saw everyone run to meet the man and greet him with bows—women and children together.

He was a tall, well-built man. He asked me my name. The other children clustered around to tell him. Some of the children wanted to help take off his shoes; others were promising to massage his body and fingers. At the end, he gave us 25 francs CFA† so we could buy some candy. And every evening, everybody dressed up to wait for his return. Mornings and afternoons, we helped him to push his ailing Vélosolex for a few meters before it decided to start.

The man was a salaried worker in an enterprise, but he also had a woodworking shop at home. His wives took turns doing the cooking every other day and spent the rest of their time with him. At noon, the menu hardly ever changed: it was always *ceeb*. The *borom-kër* ate at a fixed time, and the meal must not be too hot. The wife of the day waved a fan first so he wouldn't burn himself eating and then wiped his forehead with a handkerchief. He was shaven and manicured as well. Stretched out on a folding chair with a cushion, he let his feet soak, angled like the letter V. When the treatment was finished, he placed his feet on a wife's thigh and waited for someone to dry them.

*The brand name of a French motorbike of limited power.—*Trans.*

†CFA: the "franc CFA" (Communauté financière africaine, African financial community) is the basic monetary unit of the independent countries (former French colonies) of West and Central Africa (this monetary zone was later extended to the Indian Ocean and the Pacific and has now been integrated with the euro).—*Trans.*

None of his daughters went to school. They had to remain home to learn how to "care for and keep" their future husband, he said.

Always pleasant with the children of other people, he proved to be very harsh with his own sons. Those who were sent home from school went to the woodworking shop. Because he was energetic, he thought his own sons never worked enough. When he was angry, only the sight of his own mother could calm him down. She lived in the neighboring house. Everybody—co-wives, children, tenants—urged her to prevail on her son for mercy. This little old woman did not speak much. She knew how to go about flattering her son's pride and protecting her grandchildren.

"You are big and strong, my son. Roar when you feel like it: you are a *ndiayen*,* you bear the name of the king of the jungle. But don't expect your sons to be like you. You are a baobab. Only mushrooms can grow in your shadow!"

The son continued complaining.

"Mama, imagine! They can't manage to make the rattraps that I need to put in place! Instead of having men, I have cattle that I fatten and won't even be able to sell as sheep!"

Making rattraps must have been very important to put him in such a state. But the storm had passed, only to return again soon . . .

*A *n'diayen* is a person like N'Diadian N'Diaye, the legendary king of the Wolof, who overcame lions with his strength, courage, and majesty.—*Trans.*

We had to work hard: go to the fountain for water, empty waste water into the runoff gutters, take the garbage to the dump, go to the market . . . That's what a girl had to look forward to in this neighborhood. Parents would buy us a bucket that corresponded to our weight or, sometimes, went beyond. We could only play after dinner or at the fountain, where we had to wait for hours to get a bucket of water.

The public fountain, primarily the gathering spot for women, was the scene for quarrels, settling scores, and rivalries. Hostilities often broke out because a woman who had a turn managed to take care of the containers of one or more friends waiting at the end of the line instead of simply filling her own and getting out of the way. The women waiting impatiently in the "line" complained when this happened.

The women who jumped ahead or the ones who were especially loudmouthed had often gotten into so many quarrels that their faces were covered with scratches. This was their "lesion of honor"; it was a distinction that would let them get ahead.

Besides, other people considered the fountain as their private property. They would arrive in pairs, at least, with dozens of pans and buckets. One would monopolize the fountain by filling them while the other one took the water back to store it at the house and return with more containers. It's easy to imagine the resentment of the women who had been waiting for hours.

We girls were the fated victims of injustice by older women, who took advantage of our age to get ahead of us (it's true that we were not in a hurry to get our turn since we had so much fun with our games . . .).

I didn't understand either that the adults' privilege of age should extend to such an essential place as the public toilets. Even there, the adults pushed ahead of us.

Mama kept dreaming of moving quickly into a house with solid walls that had separate bedrooms and toilets, which for her seemed to be a luxury. But she kept arranging our room, which must have contained twenty square meters at most. The walls were papered with colorful magazine covers that should have been removed to let air pass through. Mama had a great esthetic sense. Since she was skillful with her fingers, she would embellish everything she touched.

She embroidered various sheets and their pillowcases. She crocheted bedspreads, tablecloths, napkins (she was to make a business of this) that flowered all around the house on the arms and backs of armchairs, even if they were falling apart. Nobody sat on them. At night, she preferred to take off her pretty sheets even if we had to sleep on the bare mattress. Finally, she put somber-colored pagnes on the bare mattress, complaining all the while.

"This way, the mattress won't get dirty, and my sheets will stay nice."

Mama was also compulsive about moving the furniture around. This was her way of refurnishing. After these moves, we had problems finding our way around.

"Mama, will you tell us where our stuff is?"

"You're so disorderly! A bull would get lost in this house . . ."

In irritation, Papa would answer: "Don't you think we would have at least seen his horns or his tail?"

As long as we didn't find the bed hanging from the ceiling, it was all right. Mama really wanted to change houses. This process of shifting everything gave her the illusion she was doing it . . .

Nothing could drag on with Mama. And only she could

change the order of things. She would hide anything ugly under the bed. For example, my tufts of hair that she cut often in order to make me grow. Superstitious as she was, she believed that hair and fingernails were a dangerous weapon for evil spirits. It was necessary to bury them or keep them away from enemies. But her superstitions didn't stop there. Certain actions, such as sweeping at night, were strictly forbidden. We didn't have any *kanari** or buckets of drinking water—just a water filter that was a filter in name only. It was completely white with a tap at the end. It reigned on the table. This kept some unhealthy evil spirit that Mama saw everywhere from putting something in the water or, simply, kept some bit of filth she missed in her increased vigilance from falling in.

I loved to play doctor by lining up brothers and neighbor children to give them pebbles representing pills. Mama interrupted me with a whipping in the middle of my consultation, and the patients scattered from fear of undergoing the same fate as their doctor. The pills were thrown out with a litany of incantations intended to keep any illness at a distance from the house.

The health services came by often, but within a week the fleas, bugs, cockroaches, and rats returned in force as if the disinfectants had only favored their hibernation. The *borom-kër* himself made rattraps, and each morning we would find vermin as big as cats caught in them. People laughed.

"Too bad we don't belong to the rat eaters!"

At night, we had to put on socks. Without them, we would have had our heels and toes nibbled.

Since we were kids, we had to swallow huge doses of castor oil, that slimy, ugly tasting oil, to get rid of parasites. This was as frequent and as ineffective as were the actions of the health services with the rats and bugs. You had to think these beasts led a hard life and were able to adapt to all measures taken against them.

*Earthenware jugs.

At nightfall, the only moment when we had to live in a closed space, we realized that our shack was engulfed in stifling heat. This led us to switch from one game to another to kill time. Bedtime was put off as long as possible. We began to dance the *taatu lawbe*.* We would turn a calabash over in a tub of water and drum on it, giving an impressive sound. Then we would dance around, swaying our backs and hips. We were the envy of the adults, who applauded us. Sometimes, they even joined in with us.

*Literally, the "woodcutter's buttocks," which their wives dance very well. (The dance is now called the "fan" because of the gyrations.)

The *borom-kër* tolerated dancing. On the other hand, he had forbidden fights, which always ended up in scuffles. Dance became an almost daily routine.

For a change, Kumba had dreamt up an improvised film that she took charge of projecting. A table covered with a white cloth was placed in the middle of the dimly lit courtyard. In advance, we had cut pictures out of my mother's magazines and newspapers. For lighting, we took up a collection to buy candles that our projectionist held under the table as she made the pictures turn on the white cloth. Sitting on the ground, we saw only the silhouettes moving and meeting each other. This was great fun.

Every day the number of spectators grew as other kids from the street came. If it had been a movie house, they would have been forced to put up the "sold out" sign.

We girls had prepared this cinema. We expected to keep our "places of honor," at the front. One evening there was a scuffle with intruders after the beginning. The overturned table with our pictures caught fire. We panicked, and our projectionist was slightly injured, which put an end to the showing. Our parents and the *borom-kër* were worried. Weren't we going to set fire to the neighborhood? Fortunately, the scare was greater than the damage. Parents took their children away. We went to our rooms and had to go to bed earlier than usual.

It was really hard for me to sleep in that house. I only fell into a deep sleep as the morning freshness came in.

One day, our neighbor Biram, who was often hunting for his denture, came knocking.

"I didn't want to wake you up like the last time. I found the glass of water overturned without my denture . . . after I had changed the placement of the glass . . ."

My father interrupted him.

"In that case, don't you think your denture would have been better off in your mouth rather than somewhere else?"

"The next time, I'll know where to put it. If you will allow me, I'd like to ask your children's help to find it."

He was speaking with a pathetic look as he jingled some coins in his pocket. That made us forget Mama's orders to "never get close to Biram" because she considered him a "repugnant individual" and called him a *kaña* (rat).

Without hesitation, my brother and I began looking for the denture, which we found, in fact, in a rat hole.

Although he rewarded me, Biram spoiled my sleep and made me want to vomit. With his frothy mouth, he thanked us and gave us our reward. Then he rinsed his denture and put it back in his mouth. When Mama saw this, she almost fainted and, once more, she demanded a move.

She began feverishly packing our bags, but Papa, still in control, was able to put her off by promising a move in the near future.

My first contact with the other girls happened while the courtyard was being swept in the morning. Each girl began in one corner, and we met with our brooms in the middle. We sifted the sand also. It was clean once more until the next day. The same process had to be carried out every day. That was where we consulted and laid out our plans for the day.

"We won't go fill the barrels with water this morning; we'll say that there were too many people at the fountain and that evenings are better for the job. That way, we can manage to go to the N'diago* dance," Kumba added.

What a great idea! Kumba was certainly our group leader! We would keep working hard all day long, delighted at the thought of going to our first dance . . .

*An ethnic group in the Casamance region.

That day seemed to be dragging for us and dinner unnecessary, but I had to eat in order not to raise suspicions. Each of us behaved the same way at home. Since we had to make several trips to fill the barrels, we hurried to bring back the first bucketfuls, which reassured our parents. Then we hid the buckets and headed for the dance, taking advantage of the gatekeeper's negligence.

The atmosphere was nice, and the lights were lowered. People were dancing the *pachanga* (that's what we called the salsa). They were swaying on their long, healthy legs. More often than not, they were drunk from local wine, fermented palm juice with a strong aroma and a strange taste. They were dripping with sweat. A mixture of strange odors was in the air. As for us, we were dancing, trying to imitate the older kids. But because we were so small, they quickly noticed us, and we had to leave this unsavory place that we found so attractive—but without repercussions. We went back home to get our buckets, swearing that we would go again and promising each other not to say anything about it.

Our parents didn't suspect a thing since the barrels were still full of water. We got into the habit of going back to the dance pretty often. We were no longer happy with just dancing—we would empty the bottles sitting around when we didn't actually slip right under the tables to make off with the dancers' drinks. Often it became late, and when we didn't appear, our mothers started out looking for us.

One day, they found the dance.

"Where are the buckets?"

"We hid them."

"How long have you been coming to the dance?"

"For some time."

Once we got home, we were punished royally. Kumba's mother claimed that her daughter had been dragged off by the rest of us, which gave rise to an immediate reaction from the other mothers. To listen to them, it was clear that each of us was an angel who had been led astray by the other girls.

The *borom-kër*, who had enough of our tears and the maternal quarrels, interrupted the conversation.

"We have to keep these children busy in the evening. Ali will teach them to read and count, beginning tomorrow evening. There is a large blackboard in his room (Ali was the only son of the *borom-kër* to have continued studying).

Our mothers added their agreement.

"That's an excellent idea. At their age, can you imagine? A bunch of little drunkards, habitués of the ball. What do they have in store for us tomorrow?"

They were unanimous on this point.

The dance and film performances had led me to give up my father's evening storytelling. The story I had liked most was about a prophet who had lived to the age of three hundred years.

"If I could only live that long . . ."

"Only the prophet had that good fortune," my father answered.

I was disappointed because I thought that I had a mission to carry out in life and that I would need many years to fulfill it. The prophet's age struck me as normal.

Right away, Papa gave me the name of his own parents. I knew that he had parents from another country. As for grandparents, it was the first time he had mentioned them.

"Did they have parents?"

"Of course . . . and they are dead and buried."

He gave me their names, which made them real for me and gave me a place in the family tree. But this revelation also made me recognize a sad truth: I was mortal. I wanted Papa to go as far as possible back in history to find out whether any of them had survived their mortality.

"They should have stayed with us. I would have known all of them."

"Alas, they had to die so you could be born. You know, we kept the dead among us for a long time. God put an end to that by sending two birds one day. They fought ferociously. When one of them died, the other dug a hole in the earth with beak and claws to bury the dead bird. From that day onward, humans discovered that the dead should be buried.

Getting tired of my questions, he led me back to Adam and Eve, my great-great-great grandparents.

"All right, and who were their parents?"

"They didn't have any parents; I mean, they were created by God."

"And who created God?"

"God is the Creator of the heavens and the earth and everything that is on and underneath it. He is 'Sabi sama wate walardi' (the Creator of the heavens and the earth). There is no Creator before him. And when the end of the world comes, all the dead will be resurrected and that will be the Last Judgment. Those who have done evil will be judged, and those who are pardoned will go to Paradise like children, who are angels. They will see the Prophet and God, the Creator of the Universe. That is beautiful, isn't it? And the others will burn in hell. Do you remember how I told you that each one of us has a guardian angel on each shoulder to take note of all our sins? When you ask for forgiveness, you have to say 'Astahfir Allah'*—one hundred times, which will suffice for God to forget the evil."

"I understood that, but what I do not understand is that you had parents, grandparents, and so forth, and you are telling me that God doesn't have any?"

Endless questions . . . He got up immediately. It was time for bed.

"Tomorrow, I'll tell you another story."

I didn't like for stories to end with death, and Papa always managed to avoid that ending. I was afraid to close my eyes for fear of not waking up; but, at the same time, Paradise as my father had described it attracted me. Sleep overcame me in the middle of this struggle.

---

*"Pardon, Allah."

I had been enrolled in the coranic school. A festival accompanied this beginning of an initiation. All the relatives and friends of the family came together, and I became the main attraction for the adults. All of a sudden, I was important. The coranic school wasn't far away, and my father had taken me there. I became acquainted with my first line of the Qur'an. It seemed quite serious. This wasn't the way it had been with the marabout in Rebeus. There were more boys than girls, seated on the ground in a circle in the open air, with each one reciting the lesson. But in the middle of this cacophony, the master had a keen ear. He was able to pick out cheaters making noise instead of reciting or those who were reciting the neighbor's lesson rather than their own.

The master impressed me as the shepherd of a flock; he had a stick at the end of which was a cord serving as a whip. The cord was so long that it couldn't hurt anybody . . .

The master would place you beside him to spell each word if you pronounced it badly. He would tell his pupil to take the word apart, letter by letter. Afterward, he taught us to write that beautiful script, with its designs, its camels, and its multiple accents, which had a pleasant sound and a life of its own.

He was a good and patient master. As soon as you knew the lesson by heart, he inscribed another on your *alluwal*. He alone would read the lesson first. Then, you repeated after him and he would place your index finger on each word. The third time, you had to read what you had learned. He would go back over any word you tripped on. Then you could leave. You had an interest in learning the next day's lesson because he pinched the laggards very hard.

I liked to go to the coranic school every afternoon, except Wednesday, which was a day of rest; my friends, who were not enrolled, went along with me. The master allowed them to come and had them read the *alluwal* line by line. When they saw this, their parents ended up enrolling them.

When we came home, Papa made it a rule to have us recite our lessons, and he even went ahead to the next one. After that, he taught me to write and to translate the sura or any narrative in the hadith.* This was the thing of which he was most proud. Contrary to the claims of some obscurantists, there exists no sura or any hadith narrative that denies a girl the right to know and to work. But our mothers, who preferred to have

---

*The sura are chapters of the Qur'an; the hadith are narratives of the Prophet. [Both words are attested in English.—*Trans.*]

us help with the housework full-time, began to say, "Knowing the prayers is enough for women."

After that, my friends only came when their mothers let them. As for me, I didn't have any way out of either home chores or school work. Each task was added to the other. In this respect, each of my parents expected me to do my best.

In was this little rigid but protected universe, secret and fiercely free, that the knife of the excisionist had cut off for me.

Life began again. And in a relatively carefree way. My friends and I would have liked to have those little pimples in place of our flat children's breasts. Popular belief had it that the appearance of breasts was promoted by black ants. We hunted some out in the sand and carefully placed them on the critical spots. The little beasts' stings produced a negligible swelling. It didn't hurt—it just tickled.

We kept close track of this transformation. We would touch and let ourselves be touched. The illusion only lasted an instant, and we had to begin all over. Afterward, we were no longer sure whether it was really the pleasure caused by contact with these little beasts that made us continue, or whether it was really just the desire to have breasts.

Our "bathroom" was made of fencing that formed an enclosure in the courtyard. Inside this enclosure, a large stone with pebbles spread around it served as a seat. Kumba "involuntarily" glimpsed the nudity of adults inside. She got us together right away to tell us about what she had seen and what we had to do to get the same thing. This meeting was very important. Each one of us had an opinion on what we had to do. As soon as an adult or a boy came close, we stopped talking. This was almost a state secret.

Several days later, Kumba asked each of us to contribute a tuft of hair. I insisted that each one of us contribute a tuft, but the other three answered unanimously.

"With your long hair, you can cut off a tuft for each of us."

"I will only cut one for myself," I answered, worrying about punishment from my mother.

"You're an egotist! With your mane, you could cut off enough for all of us. You only think of yourself! We're not going to play together any more."

Despite my refusal to give in to their bribery, they finally decided to stay with me. Our problem was to find a solution with a night's reflection.

The next day, on the way to market, our request of the coiffeurs to give us hair cuttings was turned down. They asked what we were going to do with it. Kumba had a ready-made answer.

"We want to make pillows."

"Pillows? What an idea!"

The more time went on, the more we despaired of being like adults. I knew that Mama kept the family's tufts of hair under the bed, to ward off evil spirits. This time, I would be the enemy.

Proud of my find, I went to meet my friends. We agreed to put our plan into action the following afternoon, when the house would be empty. A great dance, the *sabar*,* was being organized in our neighborhood. Everyone would be there. Away from our parents and loose tongues, we had decided to use the woodworking shop of the *borom-kër:* the buffet was to serve as a screen and a box marked "strong glue" would do the job. One of us would stand guard to warn us if any intruders were coming, and the other two would glue hair on at the pubis. With a piece of cloth, we would manage to hide this.

When my turn came, I changed my mind. I was obsessed by the idea that it would hurt: I instinctively tensed up and put my hand over that part of my body.

"Promise you won't hurt me."

"We swear that it won't hurt. You'll see . . . It didn't hurt us . . ."

They were persuasive, but I wasn't completely at ease. I still wanted to have the same thing they had, on my hairless little pubis, so I wouldn't feel excluded and so I wouldn't be treated as a cowardly fraidy cat.

The only solution they found was for me to remain seated, instead of lying down, so I could see what they were doing, but there was no way I could escape. This idea was all right with me because, since the excision, I wanted to be sure about the intentions of any hand that came close to my intimate parts. I let them do their work, while holding onto the hand of Sarah, who was doing the operation. I was reassured that way.

Afterward, we were happy . . . we were like adults. We had run to Kumba's room where there was a big chest with a large mirror. Each of us took a turn in front of the mirror in order to admire this gift from "God"; when one girl took too long admiring her full face and profile in front of the mirror, she was

---

*A very erotic Senegalese dance. [The *sabar* is a tam-tam, open at the bottom.—*Trans.*]

immediately pushed aside, ejected by a companion anxious to examine herself.

The people coming back from the *sabar* were surprised to see us at home. Usually, we were the first ones to run to the dance in order to have a good place. But this time, we were so happy with the success of the operation that the atmosphere of the *sabar* was no great loss. However, things were going to get complicated during the evening. I had noticed that when I pulled on the hair, it didn't come off. It hurt!

My friends said the same thing. Our uneasiness began to grow. We didn't know what to do. We would have liked to confide in someone, in our mothers, for example, but what a risk of punishment!

Kine had started sniffling, a sign of tears to come. This was irritating, but we preferred listening to this slight noise rather than having her collapse. That would have attracted attention, and it would have gone on for hours.

Our fathers were usually far from suspecting what we were capable of doing; as for our mothers, they would often close their eyes at certain stupid little things, but we knew that this time they would not forgive us for having touched that taboo part of our bodies.

At dinner time, I was nervous as I sat on a low bench, facing my mother's questioning look. I lowered my eyes. Too late . . . my short dress had given me away! My mother was staring at a specific spot, between my legs! In the seconds it took for her to rub her eyes and make sure that she had really seen some hair, I had anticipated her reaction and reached the door.

Mama interrupted her meal and went to my friends' mothers to tell them what she thought she had seen. They asked her whether she was feeling all right. Each of them swore she had seen her daughter naked that morning or the evening before and had noticed nothing unusual.

"When could this hair have grown? At their age!"

At my mother's insistence, my friends were trapped. Their mothers were speechless at what they had just discovered, while I was hunted down and led forcibly back to the house.

They took us to the maternity clinic, Le Repos Mandel, in a column of taxis. Our mothers roused a bunch of women in white smocks. We were forced to lie on a table and kept motionless. I was yelling with all my strength—the image of the excision came back to mind, and these damned hairs wouldn't come off!

Our mothers wanted to know whether we were still virgins. The women reassured them we were.

"Don't tell us that to reassure us! With these girls, we've been ready to hear the whole truth, and for some time now! Please don't give us false assurances!"

"No, we would have told you; that's part of our job!"

During the return home (we had to go on foot while we were hoping for a taxi just for the rare pleasure of getting into a car), our mothers were intrigued to find out where we had seen adults naked . . . and who it was. Who had dared expose herself to children? What else had that person done with us? They imagined it was someone of the masculine gender. They questioned us persistently. We remained mute.

We didn't see anything wrong with what we had done. Adults had pubic hairs, why not us? What link was there between virginity and our miserable little pubes?

"The next time you touch that part of your body, you'll find out it isn't a toy," Mama scolded. "I'll have old 'Red-Eyes' come to take you back to the excisionist."

"Red-Eyes!" Anything but her. This was the name of the fat woman who had come after me one sinister morning at the first call of the muezzin . . .

Like many parents, Mama spent two days and two nights standing in line in front of the school to see that I was one of the first girls enrolled. The school was in La Medina, across from the Tilène market. The number of children was limited to sixty-two per class. Each child must have reached the seventh birthday and, if not accepted that year, was refused the following year because of being too old.

Background was important; both boys and girls compared schools without knowing them. The boys, budding little phallocrats, maintained that "a school where there were only girls could not be a good one while, in ours, the mixture would help them."

We objected to that because, since our infamous dance, we attended Ali's courses every evening. We could read, write, and count better than the boys. To end this argument, we proposed to read from the well-known work *Mamadou et Bineta,* and Ali would be the referee. When the boys lost, they wanted to make trouble. They were poor losers. One of the few times we got along was when they taught us to play checkers or cards. They had made the checker board in the woodworking shop; as soon as we began to play better than they did, they began cheating and finally wouldn't play with us any more.

"We wonder what you can do other than playing with your rag dolls," they said.

They would maliciously grab our dolls and make footballs of them. We had made them ourselves. A battle followed. As soon as one of us was attacked, the others came to her defense. By means of this sacred unity, we thought we were invincible!

Our group was to go the girls' school, but unfortunately for Kumba, who was the best pupil among us, her father remained allergic to education for girls. As long as the lessons were at home, he went along with it. But in this case, we could do nothing but cry with her.

As for my mother, going to school meant gaining access to a different world. She bathed me and, taking advantage of my father's absence, she had me drink some blackish holy water, which I detested as much as castor oil, and then rubbed the rest over my body as if an initiation rite were taking place. The next morning, she repeated the same process. This time, she even removed my *dibe* to polish them, and she undid my two long braids and attached two pompoms with ribbons.

I tried on a flowing white dress with a matching skirt that I immediately decided to spread so the nice embroidery would show. I didn't understand that you were supposed to hide such a beautiful thing. I also had some black moccasins. Mama thought the plastic shoes were just for the ghetto, like wearing pagnes. For her, there were clothes for staying at home, for going to market, and for feast days.

She put away my new bookbag, which I opened and closed, examining each object several times. In order to keep it shiny, I wiped it with a cloth on which I had put a bit of oil. I placed it in front of me, and then even carried it around in order to see how it would look.

"I am going to take you to school. When your name is called, you must answer, 'Present.'"

After covering the distance on foot, we finally reached the school. A middle-aged *tubaab*,* nicely dressed and coiffed, greeted us authoritatively with a list in her hand.

"See that lady, she is the principal. If you get into trouble, she will send you away; you must promise me not to get into quarrels."

"OK, but if someone bothers me, I have to defend myself, don't I?"

"Of course, that's true. I've always told you to give back what you receive."

I wanted to tell her that I'm sometimes the one to make trouble. Anyway, what good would it be to explain to her what the ghetto is like—she didn't know. She lived in it without understanding it. How can you know what the ghetto is like when you haven't experienced the public fountain?

Mama mentioned the names of several children who had been expelled from the school.

"You won't do that to me, will you? Those children become delinquents. I'm not talking about the ones who are sent away because they can't do the work. They expose themselves to the worst misfortunes of life. The little beggars you see have been to school at some time. Some of them get along by stealing before they become real criminals—if they don't die first. School supplies that have been free up to now will have to be paid for from now on. Your school uniform is expensive, and we'll have to buy a new one each year. It's difficult to pay for children's education, you know. What do you do when you have a large family? Everything is expensive, and education becomes a luxury. Imagine, in certain schools the teachers and even the

*A white foreigner.

principals have to be bribed to get them to enroll your children so that being there early doesn't count. It's shameful! The few schools built since independence are private. If you were thrown out, we couldn't afford to pay your tuition at a private school. You can see that your father hasn't come to accompany his eldest daughter on a day as important as her first day of class. And if it were only up to him, you wouldn't have been enrolled. I'm telling you all this so you will think about it—or else, good-bye education!"

For the first time, I felt that Mama was concerned about my future. Leaving aside her attitude as a strict mother who usually terrorized me, she was imploring me. I appreciated the attention she was suddenly giving me, but I thought about Papa, who, the night before, had massaged my head and recited sura from the Qur'an before he left me alone with Mama.

"I have confidence in you," he had whispered. "Don't ever forget that. And remember what you have learned: the alphabet will be like the first line of the Qur'an for you. Everything is there and turns around that. That is the basis of all learning, whether it is in Arabic, French, or another language."

Papa was taking evening courses. When he came back to the house, he was determined to teach me all that he had learned. And we went over what Ali had taught me.

Thinking only about my father, I wasn't even listening to my mother any longer. She tapped me on the shoulder when my name was called, which made me jump, and I forgot to say "present" as I walked toward the principal. I was a dreamy, absent-minded pupil. My mind would wander in all directions. I would think of different things and facts that, at first glance, had nothing to do with one another. I had to be brought back to reality.

All the girls from our neighborhood were there. Some girls came from the well-to-do neighborhoods. They were a year younger than we were. According to Mama, they had gone to preschool, and she added that she was sure they didn't know as much as I did.

The classroom was spacious, with large glass windows that let the light come in. The very high wall was decorated with engravings. There were four long rows with two pupils at each seat.

As soon as the limit was reached, the teacher designated four larger girls to whom he gave the title of *gaillardes*,* telling them to go to the rear of the classroom.

My seatmate was a big girl, chubby, with a dark ebony complexion, contrasted with the white of her owl's eyes and her protuberant teeth. She took a disliking to me at first glance. She marked a vertical line on the desktop to show the boundary between us and, of course, she took the larger part of the territory for herself.

The other pupils and I religiously followed the teacher, who had begun the lesson in absolute silence. My neighbor, with her teeth bared, ready to bite, only paid attention to the desk. In a moment of distraction, was I going to cross the line? She would call me to order with a poke of her penholder. Her world was as narrow as her mind.

The bell rang for recess.

With its flamboyants and palm trees, the schoolyard was remarkably clean. There wasn't a scrap of paper on the ground. I found everything marvelous, and I was quite happy to be there. We studied and played peacefully, without anyone reminding us that there was housework waiting to be done at home.

I was to discover that I was sharing the desk with Patapouf. She was taking this year over, and most of the repeaters acted the same way with the new pupils. They called us the "little ones." I thought about my mother's advice, but if I had to share my desk with this girl who communicated only by pokes of her penholder, I was bound to react!

At the sound of the bell, we lined up in front of our respective classrooms and, in a line, went back into the classroom, where my fascination with the teacher went on. For me, the time went too quickly. I wished every day would be a school day. How I loved studying! This habit has stuck with me.

The teacher spoke to us.

*Wenches.—*Trans.*

"You are placed in alphabetical order now, but soon it will be by height. Every month, there will be a composition, and from then onward, you will be placed by merit. The good pupils will be in front, the average ones in the middle, and the poor ones in the back. Only the *gaillardes* will stay where they are, regardless of performance. From the moment you enter the schoolyard to when you leave, French will be the only language. You have one week to get accustomed to this. You must speak and write correctly. One mistake will get two raps on the fingertips or on your palms—depending on the nature of the mistake.

He opened his desk drawer and surprised us by taking out a long stick that he held up to us before laying it on the desk.

"As for the pupils who make too many mistakes, the four *gaillardes* will take hold of them, one for each arm and leg. I shall unstintingly apply the stick to their bare buttocks until I get tired. But well before we get to that point, I am confident that the rules of grammar and spelling that I teach you will put a limit to the number of punishments. The substitute for the rod will be to recopy the rules one hundred times and to put them into practice the next day before class begins. And then, many pupils get sleepy in the afternoon. It is known that 'a full stomach makes a sleepy kid.' In such cases, the neighbor will give a hefty slap to the sleeper. And if she fails to do that, I will do it for the two of them! Enjoy your meal, my children!"

This warning put a chill on the classroom, and dismay was apparent on our faces. We began to fear the rod. We thought about our behinds. The sound of the noon bell was welcome.

Back at the house, questions flew from all sides. I answered without mentioning the pokes with the penholder that had come all morning or what the teacher had warned us about.

I was confident because of what Papa had told me: "Everything depends on the alphabet."

The one good thought was that I was going to get rid of Patapouf! She was really on my mind, but I consoled myself with the determination to perform better than she would.

In the afternoon, several pupils did not return. As time

passed, we understood the rules about learning and discipline better. At home, we did our homework with Kumba's help, assisted by her brother Ali.

There was a reception at school. We were allowed to bring someone. We invited Kumba. Everyone spoke French to her.

"What school do you go to?"

"My father refuses to send me to school."

We were uncomfortable. We had hoped at first that the teachers would meet her and, seeing her level of intelligence, would help her. It did not happen, and we were quite disappointed. When we went home, she always worked with us. She waited for us when we got to our little street and carried our book bags. When we had to recopy lessons for our mistakes, she would do them with us.

Kine and I could help each other.

When we made an ink blot, we used a blotter and some white chalk. Sarah, who was always very careful and persistent, never managed to finish the recopying assignment. She would take a new sheet of paper for the least spot. The next day, she would get another punishment—recopying the corrected mistake one hundred times.

The word "punishment" was never articulated at home, and our parents did not understand. To them, this meant that we had not done our work properly and that, as a result, an additional punishment was inflicted on us. Without realizing it, we were the pioneers, bearers of all their hopes, since we were the first generation to go to the French school.

Every Friday and Monday morning, the principal would visit the different classes to see whether we had clean fingernails, without nail polish, and combed or braided hair. Our dresses were pulled up so she could see the underwear. We underwent strict inspections. If any rule of hygiene was not respected, we were sent home, and the parents were summoned. Any tardiness or, worse, absence had to be justified not with a signed slip, but by a visit from the parents. Generally, parents did not like to come in and if, by a child's fault, the parents were called in, the guilty party could be sure to get a whipping.

In order to be readmitted, fictive parents were often brought in to the teacher, and the fact that he would be taken in made us laugh afterward.

Every morning, Kine would leave us close to school and go to poke around Tilène market. She would usually return before the gates were closed. Not seeing her come in one day, we began to worry. The teacher had finished calling the role when we saw her come in with a gentleman she introduced as her father. The teacher explained to him that Kine was often late and that he must do something about it. This gentleman took off his ample boubou and his hat, hung them on the nail by the door, and, with great assurance, called the four *gaillardes*. Kine was beaten by this crazy man, in spite of her protests that he was not really her father. The teacher paid no attention—he must have been thinking that children often refuse to recognize their father in such circumstances. This temporary father had taken his role too seriously—he put his boubou back on and spoke to poor Kine.

"This is not over. We will take care of the rest at the house."

Holding his hat with his left hand, he spoke to the teacher with a broad smile.

"Please don't hesitate to keep me informed of any absence or misbehavior in school."

That is the way our morning began. The teacher threatened Kine with another punishment if he heard her whimper.

We all felt sorry for her. At recess, we asked Kine to tell us what had happened, although we had already guessed.

"I asked that man to pretend to be my father. I was late and afraid that . . ."

She began sobbing again. It was painful to sit down.

"It's too bad this happened to you! We won't talk about it at home," Sarah decided.

"I promise," I answered. "Try to hold up in class because the teacher won't hesitate to make good on his threat."

We were such good friends that if each of us could have taken part of the punishment to lighten her pain, we would have done it. We were lucky enough to be in the same class although there were two classes at that level. We did everything together.

"I can't even sit down—my buttocks are burning," Kine repeated. "I did what Tene told me—I sat first on one side and then on the other."

At home, Kine's behavior caught the attention of her parents. She finally told them what had happened. Sarah and I confirmed what she said. Our parents asked whether we could recognize the unknown gentleman.

"Of course," we answered.

With the *borom-kër*, our parents went looking for the man. We were ready to help them, but we changed our minds when we discovered that they intended to congratulate the stranger for "having fulfilled his duty as a father for a child who had behaved badly . . ."

That afternoon, Kine's parents came to school to meet the teacher and, undoubtedly, to congratulate him since they had not found the unknown gentleman. Kine's story made the rounds—there were fewer tardy arrivals and even absences. But the teacher made sure from then on to ascertain the identity of parents who were presented to him.

Our school was an officers' training school in which every good teacher had to prove himself. Inspectors often appeared unexpectedly. The institution had the reputation of being the best for instruction and discipline. But there was a "jungle" unknown to all officials: we were subjected to the racket of the repeaters—their intimidation and their blows. These were girls who had become hardened from their failures, and we had to pay the price in return for some peace. The only children who escaped this were those privileged to have a chauffeur or a servant accompanying them. They were there for the quality of education. For most of them, this was the first time they had mingled with people from the ghetto.

The most unfortunate victim was little Aïda, a *gurmet*.* She came to school wearing white stockings. Her well-oiled hair smelled scorched from ironing. She had a part on the side that made her head look huge. To listen to her, you would have taken her for a *tubaab* except that she rolled her *r*'s and made some incorrect liaisons that the teacher picked up repeatedly. She was Patapouf's favorite target. When the latter attacked her, Aïda would break into tears and say that it was uncivilized to fight.

But Aïda wasn't a saint either. She would often tattle to the teacher that we were speaking Wolof,† which she spoke with an affected accent, rolling her *r*'s like people from Gorée, the island she came from.

The constraint of speaking French left us speechless at recess. Having trouble counting in French, one girl would stop and another would continue. This was often Aïda, who spoke

*A person of the Catholic faith.
†The language of the Wolof people.

French at home. Every one of us resented this. As for Patapouf, who had a lot of trouble speaking Voltaire's language, she inevitably detested Aïda. She called her a *ciip ciip*.*

Patapouf went so far as forbidding Aïda to wear stockings, barrettes, or even to wear a part in her hair. As soon as she would get to school, she would take off her stockings, her barrettes, and even undo the part in her hair. Only on her way home could she put everything back in place. At home, a thrashing awaited her since she had often forgotten to put things in order or had done it poorly.

This intimidation was an awful situation that each of us underwent every day with methods the repeaters adopted according to circumstances.

Mama would give me a snack for the ten and four o'clock recesses. The repeaters found a way to exact their share. As often as not, they would take it all. This was also true of our school supplies. These shortages brought questions from Mama that I couldn't answer, which made her furious. Because of the terror, we sometimes regretted the teacher's rewards. We would rather have said, "No, thank you, sir—the consequences will be too serious." He would give big pieces of egg-shaped candy to the good pupils. We couldn't eat them in class—only during recess. This candy was obviously the envy of the girls who didn't get any, and their frustration made them vicious. As soon as I went to the playground, I swallowed a piece of candy too big even for my eager mouth, closing my eyes so I wouldn't see their begging or threatening eyes. I could share anything. Let them take anything, except the candy, which I considered as my own treasure meant for me alone!

I thought about Mama's recommendations. In my morning prayers, the only ones I did, before reciting the Qur'an on my *alluwal* and my lessons, I asked God to help me not to falter. But the limits of my patience were quickly reached: at the least provocation, the blood rushed to my eyes and I went into a fury.

*A person who imitates to a "t" the culture of the Whites.

One day, Daba saw a key ring that I had taken from Mama. There was a little bottle on it. She asked me for it. I refused. She was surprised since it was the first time I had said "no" to her.

"Do you know who you're talking to?"

"I'd like to find out right now."

"It's recess time. When we go out, you'll discover that nobody messes with me."

"I'll be looking for you."

My determined replies threw my adversaries off. It sometimes happened that I became so quiet I didn't answer any more. Daba saw her efforts at intimidation fail, contrary to the usual fawning of her peers, the cowards and the hypocrites.

Fights took place off the school grounds. Leaving school, I found myself faced with my adversary, who was being carried by her followers so she wouldn't get tired walking. She repeated her entire speech and then thanked my friends for coming with me.

"You can help her poor mama identify her after I've finished."

She was going to tear me apart. There would be all kinds of frightful suffering. This made me think of the *làmb*.* Nothing was missing but the tam-tam.

I wanted to get it over with. We reached the spot, a veritable battlefield. The place for our disputes was a dirty, smelly vacant lot. Some enemies from the area, both boys and girls, were already at war. The onlookers were standing close, and we could hear their comments. Beginning with the first round, I lit into my adversary and threw her to the ground. She got back up and grabbed me. For the first time in my life, I was sorry I didn't have four arms.

Fortunately, during the heat of battle, some men passing took off their belts to put a stop to the fight. This caused a general stampede. I got back to the house with torn clothes and missing one shoe, but I still had my key ring.

*The spectacle of the fight.

Mama took this as the occasion to remove my *dibe*.

"That way, you're less likely to be wounded or, worse, to lose them since they're a family heirloom."

She told herself she wouldn't buy me anything else. A promise she never kept. She liked to see her children well-dressed. She understood that she had to choose: either let me defend myself like a real ragpicker or let me be crushed by the other girls.

My character was not to turn the other cheek. I couldn't help it. I was ready to stand up to anybody.

The next morning in the drawing class, one of the few subjects where Patapouf stood out and I was inept, I took the occasion to give her a hard, resounding slap. The teacher turned around.

"What is going on?"

"She's sleeping," I answered without looking at Patapouf.

"That's not true, sir, I'm not sleeping."

"All right, let's get on with the class."

Taken by surprise, Patapouf stopped drawing. She protected her cheeks, expecting another slap. I had just saved my territory on the seat, which she was taking over. As for Daba, my enemy from the day before, I managed to confront her. On the playground, lots of things took place: bumps with the shoulder, stepping on toes, pushing into a wall. This big-mouth was lost without her followers. I had learned that the only way to win the war with these terrorists was to let them know that you're not afraid of them. Kine and Sarah followed my example. We had split up our enemies.

Patapouf and her "peers" reconsidered the situation. They wanted a truce and suggested that we join their side. But I didn't want to be either a chief or a groupie. Just leave me alone, that's all!

Aïda finally managed to restore the system of justice. Tired of getting thrashings, at school as well as at home, she told on Patapouf. Aïda's mother and sisters came to school one afternoon. They were dressed completely in black and were wearing smooth wigs. One of her sisters had a red wig and fake bangs that she kept pushing back into place as she shook her head, like a real *ciip ciip*. The other sister had covered her face with shiny make-up that was too bright. Only her mother did not seem eccentric.

The teacher gave her his seat, and we went to get two others for the disguised sisters.

The proceedings began.

"I am a widow with three daughters to feed; but my little Aïda has been subjected to the racket by the persons I am going to mention to you. In addition, my daughter has been beaten by these savages who, rather than being in school, should be in their ghetto, for want of a jungle to contain them."

The law of silence was instantly broken. This was a terrific relief. For at least one hour, three quarters of the class denounced the five pupils who had organized the racket. Patapouf was the first. The denunciation went beyond our class. There was a whole network. As soon as Aïda's family had left, the teacher spoke to the racketeers.

"Tomorrow, you will come with your parents.

Leaving school, they were booed.

Over the following days, the teachers and the principal met to deal with the scourge, with the possibility of expelling those responsible for this "gangrene." Because of these girls, some children had left school.

They were not expelled. But in this system of selective education, a class can be repeated only once. Patapouf and her gang were destined to be left aside.

One day I fell ill.

I lost consciousness, and when I woke up, I found myself in Le Dantec Hospital, Dakar's big health-care center. I was in the care of some good French sisters who gave me books and dolls, reassuring me that everything would be all right. Taking advantage of my delight, they applied some hot compresses on my painful buttocks in order to make the swelling from multiple shots go down. Fearing my father wouldn't come back to visit, I accepted the shots and compresses. This was the traditional extortion: accept the shots or no visits. I wanted to have my father and my uncle Balla visit. I was waiting impatiently for my father's visit.

He took a walk with me in the courtyard of the hospital. I was happy because I had all his attention for myself. He went on talking about life outside.

The good sisters read with me and played games too. I was with them more than with children my age. They kept asking me to recite. They were a good audience. I would change voice and gesture according to which character I was playing, just as in class.

"Have you acted in plays or gone to the theater?" they asked.

"No!"

"Who taught you to recite the way you do?"

"I hear my teacher imitate characters from comedy, and I like that!"

I was sorry to leave the good sisters, but I had enjoyed seeing my first Father Christmas, who, to top it off, was a black man. He gave me a doll. That was the first time I had something all my own.

The sisters encouraged me to go to the radio station once I

left the hospital and to appear on a broadcast of recitation and singing.

So I asked my father to tell me where the radio station was. I wanted to know if it was far from where we were living. He answered without paying much attention when I would have liked for him to ask me some questions. As for my mother, I had decided to keep my distance. During my two months in the hospital, she had only come to see me once. Yet, she was smiling and seemed glad to see me. Maybe this was because of the housework, which wouldn't be long in starting up again. In the meanwhile, I allowed myself a day off on Thursday morning. I was prepared for the consequences that I supposed would follow. I had decided to go to the radio station. The evening before, I had chosen my dress and ribbons, and I wanted to wear my moccasins, just like the first day of school. The shoes were a problem. How could I take them without Mama realizing?

Only Kumba could lend me her shoes without attracting attention from her parents, but she had big feet. We put some newspaper inside to make them fit and I began to practice walking before the fatal day. Early in the morning, I asked my brother to go with me. He had gone by Kumba's place to pick up the things in a plastic bag.

From La Medina to the radio station, in the center of town, was quite a walk. We followed the bus route, asking directions along the way. This was the first time we had gone so far. At the station, we were impressed by the building over which a flag was floating and by the gendarme at the entrance. Afraid he would not let us in, I spoke to my brother.

"Let me dress properly before we speak to the gendarme."

With him shielding me, I dressed in the street. My ghetto clothes, as my mother called them, went into the sack. My brother helped me close the zipper on my dress, fix my hair, and tie my ribbons, something I had never been able to do. I took a few steps in my oversized shoes in order to gain my composure. It was torture! I had taken out some of the newspaper, but my toes were still cramped and in pain.

My brother burst out laughing as he imitated my duck walk.

I went to speak to the gendarme with a big smile. He was looking at my shoes. (This image was to come back years later when I was auditioning for a fashion parade and had to wear high heels. The selector looked at my book, then glanced directly at my bird legs. I asked him if he did not like the color. We broke out laughing, which got me the job!)

With surprising assurance, I spoke to the official.

"Good morning, Mr. Gendarme. I have been sent by my school to go on the *Uncle P.* show."

"That doesn't begin until ten thirty, and it's not yet nine o'clock."

"That's all right, I'll wait."

"You can wait inside."

"Thank you, but I'll wait outside and come back at ten o'clock."

I was afraid to go in with my brother, who would continue making fun of me.

I went back to my brother. I began to recite "La Petite Fille" by Victor Hugo.

"What do you think?"

His only answer was to begin reciting in a nasal, stammering voice.

I was determined not to let myself be discouraged by this nuisance. I went back to the gendarme, who let me go in. At ten o'clock, several girls came in. There were five of them. The host came in. He was a jovial gentleman and explained what the broadcast was about. Each person had to use the microphone on the stand without touching it.

"You know, all Senegal will be listening to you beginning at two o'clock. Now we can begin."

There was complete silence.

From that moment on, I didn't think about my brother, who might leave without me, or about my mother, whom I could imagine being already at the police station to report her children missing. I concentrated on reciting. It went well, and at the end I told the host that I would return the following week. I enjoyed it . . .

I was in a hurry to get rid of those shoes. As for my brother, who had not been allowed into the studio, he was playing alone with the marbles he always had. I was glad to find him there. I put my own clothes and shoes back on, and we went home without a worry. The road back seemed shorter. As we entered our little street, everyone began interrogating us.

"Where were you? We looked everywhere for you."

Our parents were worried and the neighbors too. We saw the serious look on Mama's face. I didn't want to explain (an attitude that later cost me friends), but my brother explained for both of us, as usual.

"You know, Mama, we went to the radio station and at two o'clock, you have to listen to 'us.'"

"I'm too upset to punish you. I would give you such a whipping that your own father wouldn't recognize you."

But the word "radio," that magic word, put her in a good mood once more. And as if by magic, all the neighbors knew where my brother and I had gone and that, at two o'clock, they were going to hear "us." Mama decided to go shopping then. As she went, she told everyone willing to hear that they must listen to the radio: her children were supposed to speak at two o'clock. She came back and quickly began to cook. My brother and I were very hungry because our last meal had been dinner the night before.

"Radio-trottoir"* worked marvelously. It wasn't yet one o'clock when a crowd began gathering in the courtyard of the house to listen to Mama's radio, which we were hoping would work without any problem.

This wealth, which we were the only ones to have, this extremely rare gadget, made the neighbors marvel. Adults borrowed it when it wasn't the whole building that gathered in the courtyard to listen to it. This radio was infested with cockroaches, bugs, and other creatures. In order to make it work,

---

*Word of mouth.—*Trans.*

Mama would tap on it several times in a way that only she knew. The radio did its job, obeying her every command just as her children did.

Mama gave it the usual treatment of taps so it would be ready to speak right on time. Seeing the crowd, my father thought the worst had happened. Without waiting for him to ask, people told him the news.

My stomach was all knotted up and I thought, "If the broadcast doesn't come on at two o'clock, for whatever reason, it will be a catastrophe."

Just before time, the miracle happened! The radio started working and the program began. Everybody was listening. When my turn came, I held my breath, squeezing my brother's hand very tightly. After listening to me, people didn't listen to the others on the program. They wanted to hear my piece again. Some of them turned the radio around to look behind, as if they were looking for me.

"Too bad we can't see you. What's a radio station like? What do you speak into? Where do you stand? How is it that you went on at ten thirty and are just getting the broadcast now?"

Quite pleased, my parents smiled broadly at the crowd, thanking them all for coming to the event. When the people who were there left, others who had heard the broadcast at home or at a neighbor's made it their duty to come congratulate me. There was a great hubbub: the volume had been turned up so everybody could hear, and people were speaking endlessly and very loudly, which I hate. This was a guaranteed headache for me. Later, I would appreciate my grandmother who said, "When the radio is on, you lower your voice or you keep quiet."

I only ate later; then my father questioned us.

"How did you get to the radio station?"

"On foot," my brother answered.

"I hope that you will have transportation and will be better dressed when you go back."

With a dignified, haughty look, my mother gave no sign of

emotion. All she said was, "How could you go to such an important place dressed in rags? This really makes me ashamed."

People kept asking me constantly about the broadcast—it was the topic for all my friends, who wanted to do what I had done. I was hoping that my fame would last only a day and that the next day would be different. At school, I was practically attacked. The sound of the bell put me at ease, but in class the teacher joined the crowd. He congratulated me, saying that he hoped to hear me the next time and that, during recess, he would like for me to stay in and to describe the radio station to him! He forgot to collect the penalty homework.

This radio broadcast really fascinated everybody. For them, the mysterious thing was how to get on the program. In fact, you just had to be there early, since only a limited number of children could participate, and to know what you were going to recite.

This created some friction with my friends; there was a mixture of envy and jealousy. They were reproaching me for something vague, for not being the same person since I came out of the hospital. At times I felt distant from them, although, in front of other people, they defended me body and soul.

I went back to the radio station a lot. The host stopped me one day.

"You know, you have to let other children have a chance."

"I came without eating anything and I worked all week on my recitation, with my teacher's help."

This was true.

"I'll let you recite. What are you going to do for us today?"

" 'Le Corbeau et le Renard,'* and I'm even going to sniff the cheese."

"OK, but promise me you won't come back next time and that you'll write to tell me how your studies are going."

I was sad, but a bit relieved. As soon as I got home, where people were waiting for me, I announced that I wasn't going

---

*"The Crow and the Fox," La Fontaine, *Les Fables*, Book I, ii.— *Trans.*

back, with no explanations. My parents were disappointed. As for my friends, I had expected things would return to normal, but they were unhappy that I had given up. I couldn't understand them. I explained only to the teacher why I was not going back to the station.

"That's too bad, you know. Every Thursday, my family, neighbors, and friends were coming to hear my pupil recite. I was very proud of you. They even wanted to meet you. Too bad!"

After the move to La Medina, my father kept running his store in Rebeus. Then he put Balla, one of his brothers, in charge of the store, and it went into bankruptcy. Mama was outraged.

"Why not say that your brother worked in his own interest rather than talking to us about bankruptcy?"

In Mama's presence, I didn't dare speak about this uncle, whom my brother and I liked. He had been raised by my father. He was a hardened bachelor, interested only in married women. In order to calm him down, my father threatened to go to the village to find him a wife against his will. Years later, that's what he finally did so his brother would not die a childless bachelor (it was impossible to recognize the daughter he had with a married woman). This was the greatest catastrophe in my uncle's life. He had all the problems in the world with his wife. What he had told us was true.

"I'll never marry a woman from the village, because as soon as she gets to town and can tell a door from a window, the problems begin."

Sometimes, my uncle, an amateur boxer, would take my brother and me to training sessions. I returned home more tired than the boxers because of dodging or taking blows from the adversaries. He wasn't willing for me to go with him any longer to this masculine sport that I hated. In fact, it made me ill to see him injured (but I was also proud of him whether he won or not). I felt safe with him. He was the only one who congratulated me on my successes at school and gave me presents.

On the feast of Aïd-el-Khebir,* my brother Laye and I were waiting for Papa to return with a fat sheep. Each child was proud to show off the family sheep. We didn't have one to show off. Still worse was that Papa had become the butcher for all the surrounding households. As a reward, he got the skin and some pieces of meat. He would dry and tan the skins, sprinkling them with ashes.

Mama was beside herself. She shut herself in the bedroom and refused to accept anything from others.

Papa tried to explain.

"Do you want me to go steal something to please you?"

And without waiting for a reply, he went on.

"I won't do it, not even if we are in extreme need, but nobody will come the day after the feast to exact payment for a debt that I haven't been able to honor. That, and not poverty, would bring shame. We are not going to incur debts—that's a matter of dignity and pride. If we really had to do it, the debt would have to be a life-and-death matter, and it would have to be reimbursed as soon as possible. That's how I was raised. It's already pretty good if I leave you with no debts when I die."

Days after feast days were difficult, and people were sated after stuffing themselves with meat. Meat consumption was unusual because of the price and the eating habits of this city located on the shore of an ocean full of fish.

We quickly forgot there were still no toilets in this makeshift shack that served us as a dwelling. Big tomato cans were kept and polished to serve as chamber pots. In the morning, very early, as if everybody had agreed on the time, the contents

---

*This feast commemorates the day when Abraham tried to sacrifice his son, Isaac, who was replaced by a sheep.

could be quietly emptied into the gutters. Often a watchman was there before the offenders. In that case, you simply had to change directions and go to the public toilets. An antipathetic employee from the health department was there too. He was stubborn as a mule. He wanted to make a big show of being the master of the place and would send you away without letting you empty the pot, the discreet task for which you had been made to get up early. Adults, women in particular, went out of their way simply to yell at this gentleman. The only answer he would give was to hold his nose and grasp his *bolde*** when he felt he was facing somebody more formidable than himself.

*A large staff in the shape of a cane with a knob.

Papa attracted people. There were always people around him. It was not clear how and where he became acquainted with them. He was humorous about everything. He said that if he had gone to school, he would have been holding the office of the president of the Republic. He admired President Senghor, who was a model for him. Uncle Balla was quick to respond.

"Fortunately that did not happen, *koto*!* Can you see us in that huge palace? We'd be bored to death! And besides, to talk to you, I'd need an interpreter."

Papa preached the Good Word and found solutions for the problems of other people. Considering the number of people who came to see him, he must have been an "enlightened man, much listened to," although he couldn't understand his own problems. He gave adults instruction on the Qur'an, practical advice on actions to take, behavior that might spoil ablutions and make prayers ineffectual or sacrilegious. When I was there, they used metaphorical expressions in their questions to keep me from understanding anything.

My father also had some rudimentary skills of a health assistant thanks to his French friends, the military of the colonial period. They had left him a white, wooden case on which there was a red cross. Our room had been transformed into a shot clinic. His patients must have had venereal diseases for which they did not want to go to the hospital, whether from shame or poverty.

After they left, Mama would double the amount of Clorox she used to disinfect the room. She saw microbes as large as Sahel tribesmen.

I became Papa's assistant, as Mama said ironically. I boiled

*Big brother. [This is a Peul word.—*Trans.*]

needles in a saucepan that Mama gave him so he wouldn't touch any of the spotless kitchen utensils. The saucepan had been used so much that it wasn't necessary to wash the outside any longer, which didn't bother the patients.

Usually, Papa "forgot" to ask for payment. In fact, it bothered him to ask for what he was owed. That wasn't the important thing for him; human contact and the satisfaction of having given service were enough for him. For example, he asked one of his patients, a fish vendor by trade, to pay him in fish if he couldn't afford 150 francs C.F.A.

I was to take advantage of father's customers and patients by giving reading lessons.

While father charged 150 francs, I asked for double the fee and went to their homes if they paid my bus fare extra.

Papa thought this was scandalous, and he spoke to me about love of humanity and the giving of oneself, of good actions that God would reward a hundred fold. That didn't mean anything to me. I didn't listen to him. I was earning more than he did. He was happy to get a "God will reward you" instead of his fee.

Teaching adults to read seemed to me simpler than teaching them to tell time. Many people wore nice watches without knowing how to use them. Tapha, for example, didn't know how to tell time unless the face of the watch had Arabic instead of Roman numerals.

I drew watch faces and explained that the placement of the hands with whatever watch gives the same result. Tapha refused to let me teach his wife to tell time and asked me not to show him in front of her.

"I'll come to you. You know, I'm the one who tells my wife the time. As for learning to read, you can come to our house as we agreed."

"What? You tell your wife what time it is?"

"I don't make mistakes between noon and midnight. But before noon, for example, I tell her it's 'before ten o'clock,' 'before eleven o'clock,' or 'half past.'"

"But how much 'before,' and 'half past what'?"

"That's not important—she repeats what I've said to the other women. I'm her husband, right?"

With him, things always went slowly. He would interrupt often to try to stump me.

"Do you know what seventeen o'clock or zero hours means?"*

I had to answer his questions first and continue reciting, B . . . A, . . . BA. His vanity made him want to rush. One day, he told me, "I've found somebody who explained to me in record time what thirteen hundred hours and fourteen forty-five mean."

"I'm glad for you. In that case, we'll continue reading today."

"I'm going to leave at seventeen hundred hours—I have to go somewhere."

At sixteen forty-five, I told him the time.

"Is that past seventeen o'clock?"

"It's sixteen forty-five."

He fell silent.

Papa waited until my pupil left to speak to me.

"Don't be hard on them. Do you know that your mother and I are illiterate, like them? I had to take courses for adults and pay people in order to learn. Fortunately, there were some friends who taught me for free" (he looked at me). "In turn, I taught your mother, and she took courses to learn to read. All of this took place before you were born. I have continued to study and to improve myself."

I was shocked to hear the word "illiterate." The sound was harsh.

Mama added, "God save us from illiteracy! That's having eyes without seeing."

*Use of the French twenty-four hour clock (in which one p.m. will be given as thirteen hundred hours, and so forth) has been retained here in order to show the cause of Tapha's confusion. Zero hours refers to midnight.—*Trans.*

She took her text and read aloud as if she wanted to take her distance from ignorant people, to flee at any cost.

"I was happy to teach you to read, to write, and to count," Papa continued. "Now, I can't help you with your homework any more—I take advantage of learning from you. The pupil has gone beyond the master, and I'm very proud of that. I keep studying and teaching people the Qur'an, which I would like to know better, to possess as well as I do the Arabic language. You'll have a hard time being better than I am in that, although you're already very good."

We were experiencing a period of tension between the two heads of state in Senegal and Guinea. The Guinean nationals were paying the price of this disagreement, although it was not their concern.

Most of us Guineans had seen their offspring born in Senegal and were welcomed by the people here. Some had married in this country. This created relationships.

I had seen raids. I was unhappy, and I didn't understand everything that was happening. What I feared worst was that I might come home from school one day to find my father missing. I latched on to him when I came home from school or when he was leaving. Papa didn't want to change a thing in his daily routine. His fatalism was almost a refusal to see.

He would say: "The Earth is burning. We can't climb to heaven, can we? No, so there is only God's will. No other way!"

Mama had become overwhelmingly nervous. She had never dealt with the bankruptcy of the store. And the current situation did nothing to make things better. A certain tension was in the air. If a crack appeared in a bowl, she would give me a good slapping. And when people reacted, she would answer:

"That's an advance on the next foolish act she will soon commit. It doesn't matter that she's the eldest—if I ask for water, she will bring me fire."

If my glance met hers or I heard her voice, I was paralyzed with panic. I no longer knew what I should or shouldn't do. My knees knocked together.

Now I told myself that my parents must be expert accountants without realizing it—with my father noting our foolish acts in his little notebook and my mother giving out advances on punishment.

But I held on. The body to which she gave so many blows became an inert mass that failed to react. This exasperated her. It was our arm wrestling. I wanted to die at her hands—let her have that on her conscience, at least! The only thing that would deliver me from her power! And let me thumb my nose at my father.

As for him, he continued to live a yo-yo life. He had just set up a little vendor's table (cigarettes, cola drinks, fruit . . .). He worked in the evening, taking advantage of the street light.

The little business he had just started was the first thing he did when he came to Dakar, at ten years of age. He did not seem to understand that he was regressing—he didn't even complain. He had the idea that he would bring back to life the ambiance of his shop in Rebeus, gone forever.

That place would be invaded in the evening by gentlemen gathering at the end of their work day: patients, pupils, ousted deputies who brandished a copy of the newspaper *Paris-Dakar* to prove any argument they made. In this paper there was gossip from Paris about French politics rather than news about Senegal.

Everyone sat on long benches around our shop to engage for hours on end in ample discussion about everything and nothing. The world was made and remade, from digression to digression. As for me, I sold to the children white mice my Uncle Bala had given me. A couple of mice had reproduced very quickly. My brother Laye helped me sell them and, in particular, helped protect them from the rats that prowled nervously around the cage at night. These rats no longer wanted our heels and toes, hoping to benefit from a new menu of mice. From then on, we could sleep calmly without worrying and without putting on those famous socks to protect us from the invaders.

That little business gave me some profit in addition to the lessons I was giving. I didn't spend it—I gave it to my father. I liked to save. The same was true of the money some of the men gave me, predicting a brilliant future in which I was apparently going to make the most of everything as an adult. I would have my way with men, it seems.

Papa would give my money back to me, and my mother . . . would take it away down to the last centime. She would beat me if I resisted.

One day Mama waited for my father to leave and asked me to give her the money. I refused. She ran after me yelling, "Thief!"

When they heard her, everybody took it upon themselves to begin yelling and to catch me. If I wasn't strung up, it was only because I was a child. I landed at my marabout's place and took refuge behind him, wrapped in his great boubou. I yelled that the money was mine.

"She stole it."

Then my mother began slapping me. I held my treasure tightly. She lifted my fingers and twisted them in all directions, trying to make me let go. Afraid that she would break one or more of my fingers, I finally let go. Then I stamped on the money and spit on it. She picked it up and left, abandoning me to a gathering of people of all ages shouting their rage. That gave me a reputation as a thief, increasing the number of my enemies.

Exploited, humiliated, beaten for my work . . .

Return home.

"If I hadn't brought you into the world, you wouldn't be there, you wouldn't be earning money."

That evening, I didn't say anything to my father. Instead of selling my mice, I gave them away with the idea they would be safer with other children than if I simply let them go. I gave up every source of income, including the lessons, in spite of the insistence of my father's friends who offered to double my salary.

If someone offered me money, I quickly spent it on nonsense rather than keeping it on me. I didn't want to have any more money.

Every hiding place was discovered somehow by my mother. I could have put my money under the carpet. That would have been the day she chose to move it or turn it over! Under the mattress? She would feel it had to be turned over. It wasn't systematic searching but simply an exceedingly keen flair.

I didn't miss the money, but I was frustrated not to be teaching any more. That is how I discovered how much I liked what I was doing. That is when I discovered the importance of being useful to people older than I was.

Papa and I never spoke about my mother's violent ways. I am sure he wasn't unaware of them. Of course, he could have put an end to them. If he had not hidden his face, as he did in all circumstances.

The *borom-kër* came to remove the light bulb because the electric bill was included in unpaid rent. Mama used a flashlight at night to give a bottle to the baby.

According to the neighbors, my parents used our absence for fighting with each other. Papa broke bowls, plates, crochet hooks, needles: everything that Mama treasured most. The neighbors had enough of this and promised each other not to intervene any more. But they couldn't help it—they would come back to spy.

Sitting outside one day, I happened to overhear a conversation between my parents. Papa was answering Mama's question just as I was forced to do with him when I had done something stupid. I didn't hear that reassuring voice he had when he spoke to us. Papa had been fired, as a matter of fact, because he found it normal to stop working for prayer time. The company where he was working was run by a *tubaab* who said that he was paying his employees to work and not to pray.

The first time he found my father and his colleagues engaged in prayer, he simply warned them. The second time, he gave them a three-day leave without pay. He always gave two warnings; if workers did the same thing a third time, he threw them out.

"I think that he should let us pray at the designated times (ablutions and prayers took only ten minutes). We could begin work earlier or finish later."

"Now your prayers and coranic texts are going to feed us while we had family allocations and even a guaranteed retirement plan when you were working."

"You know, this boss fired Diogou the guard as well."

"What did he do? He is a Christian as far as I know."

"People listened to him because of his prophetic dreams, and we took him for a kind of visionary. In order to protect the boss, he related a dream that foreshadowed an accident if a travel plan were not put off."

"Then what?"

"The boss told him that he was being paid to remain awake. The boss felt that the fact he had been dreaming was more than the failure to carry out his duties, it was a serious fault. In other circumstances, he could have kept him if he had only fallen asleep. But dreaming, that was too much!"

"So how many of you were fired?"

"Three! No, four, plus the guard."

"And how many workers were there?"

"Over one hundred. We all pray, but the others hide when they do it."

"And does the *borom-kër* pray?"

"Yes, he hides to pray."

"Isn't he the one who found the job for you? Couldn't you have imitated him?"

"I can't hide to pray. I find that praying, paying homage to God, comes before everything else, and the prayer times are set with that in mind."

"Your attitude comes from irresponsibility. I am fatigued by the heavy duties of caring for this family. It is becoming more difficult all the time. I'm going to go stay with my brothers in Casamance and leave the children with you. When I was married, I came alone—I am leaving alone."

My father left without answering. He remained silent for a long time. He only noticed my inopportune presence on the bench some time later.

"What are you doing sitting there? Why don't you go play with the children?"

"I don't feel like playing any more."

Mama took advantage of father's absence to take us with her to Casamance. This was the period of our long vacation. We would travel by boat.

She left my two older brothers behind and took my little brother, my baby sister, and myself with her. Why me? I wondered about that. I was the one she punished most. I quickly discovered the explanation: she was taking me along because I was dependable help, a good worker. I never complained and, besides, I didn't say much. She needed me to bathe and diaper the kids, along with other tasks.

During the crossing, I didn't want to stay beside her—I preferred to stay at the railing looking at the sea, which stretched out of sight. The horizon made me dream of voyages far away.

We passed by only men in pirogues, which lent a picturesque aspect to our crossing. I was going to have something to tell my friends, and I was missing them already.

Mama joined me with the children to make me go back to our cabin. She was finally talking to me, while I didn't want to hear a thing. I wanted to stay where I was.

"We're going to stay with your maternal uncle; he is the elder. I've had enough of this situation; I want to get a divorce. I wouldn't like to see you growing up any longer in this atmosphere of misunderstanding with parents ripping each other apart. Unfortunately, I can't do anything without consulting him, since I'm a woman. I'll need his support. He has held the parental authority since your grandfather's death.

I didn't say a thing.

The crossing seemed too short, although it lasted three days. Nobody was there to meet us. We took a taxi to go to my uncle's place. When we arrived, there wasn't a "hello" or even a word of welcome from him.

"What gave you leave to come see me? Could it be that you have a letter from your husband?"

"No, I'm here without his permission."

An immediate family council with my other uncles was called.

"I want a separation from my husband; we don't get along any more. I'd rather not go into other details. When a mother with five children wants a divorce, it means that things are no longer going well."

"What do you reproach him with?"

"In fact, nothing particular comes to mind. I'd say that I reproach him for everything. We are too different. I have spent my time putting up with this man by doing all sorts of work to make our lives better. But the precarious situation in which we've been living doesn't bother him; he accepts it. He has almost no ambition. My first mistake was to marry this man in spite of my parents' refusal."

"You were warned that this man isn't from our class. He is a noble, of course, but with no family history; his father, a landholder, had no education or titles. This was a misalliance. Besides, how can a man be out of work when his wife is working? We have trouble imagining a woman who takes care of the family's needs. This is the world turned upside down. We will not do your husband the honor of summoning him. You are an ambitious woman who married a dream merchant, but you cannot get a divorce with five children. And there is no question of our harboring one of our sisters who talks of divorce. Only if your husband repudiates you. Then we would take you in."

They wanted to send us back to Dakar by land that very day. Mama begged them to let us spend the school vacation there. She was betting on the length of the stay, which would be three months, in order to change my uncles' minds.

While the future of my parents was being decided, I learned to ride a bicycle, climb trees, and speak the local language. I took advantage of the wide-open spaces to run all around. I wanted to dance about.

My cousin, just slightly older, took delight in throwing earthworms at me, when he didn't find snails. That made me yell until I was sick and made me break out in hives.

Another phobia came from the green spots on the walls of the bathroom. That's why I washed in the middle of the courtyard in shorts, to general disapproval. People wanted me to confront the things that scared me. Life always reserves surprises, they told me.

My cousin threatened to take off the outrageous green spots and rub them all over me. My uncle spoke to him.

"She is your fiancée!"

That put an end to his tyranny. In order to confirm our engagement, he took me to the river fishing. We brought back some live fish. I enjoyed watching them wiggle and try to escape. With him, I also benefited from some memorable falls on the bicycle. I was virtually a unique case: women rarely ride a bicycle because they run the risk of losing their virginity.

We returned to Dakar. Not directly home, but to a maternal uncle's home. Papa was alerted. He came there, knelt down to our height to hug us, without paying any attention to Mama. He came back to get us in the evening. As a matter of discretion, I suppose.

In keeping with the injunction from my uncles, Mama as a woman had to obey and return to the conjugal hearth. Nothing had changed in the ugly home situation. My brothers were busy stopping up the rat holes. This was their way of welcoming us home. I couldn't close my eyes all night. I was thinking about my parents. I hoped to see them getting along with each other once more.

In spite of having only twenty square meters of living space, Mama found a way to take in one of her friends who had been repudiated, along with her child. This was the beginning of an unending parade of gentlemen who came to visit this beautiful woman, without my father's knowledge. Papa didn't appreciate our guest's stay because she was a bad example for his wife, who became more and more independent.

The woman did not help with any of the housework or contribute to household expenses. For one of her lovers, she had some chickens roasted (a dish of honor, the caviar of the Peul). I helped the woman prepare them; once they were cooked, they were carried away, right under my nose. She gave the entire dish to her lover. She had only the legs, the head, and the entrails.

She often sent me to see him. The man would give me money or little presents that I had to hide before delivering them.

One day, my father came home earlier than usual and saw me carrying a soup bowl firmly attached with a scarf on top of my head.

"Where are you going?"

"I'm taking this meal to one of our "subscribers.""

"Since when have our "subscribers"* been getting home delivery?"

Papa had me turn around. He told Mama's friend to untie the soup bowl, which she did. He had understood what had been going on in this house. We thought that this embarrassment would make her leave, but something more was needed.

Papa gave us the chicken.

. *Bachelors who received their noon meal from us and paid at the end of the month.

Mama's friend took advantage of my parents' absence to go out, leaving her baby with me in addition to my brothers and sister. She went to her lover's place unexpectedly and found another woman there. She stabbed the woman in the stomach with scissors; by chance, the other woman did not die, but her yelling brought the neighbors in.

When the police were called, they brought the wounded woman and the betrayed mistress to our place. Our neighbors volunteered to answer questions. Everyone was against the "repudiated woman."

The police stayed until our parents came home.

We never again saw the woman who caused the trouble.

This was the time when Mama began distributing her children like loaves of bread. One of my brothers was placed with my maternal uncle in Casamance (by this means, Mama made him pay for his stubborn refusal to allow her to get a divorce). My little sister was given to one of Mama's friends who had never been able to have children—this woman also lived in Casamance. This brother and sister never saw each other, although they were living close to one another.

When my father expressed surprise about my sister's absence, mother replied in the most natural manner.

"I gave her to Tahir. Do you remember her? She lives in Casamance—this will give me some relief."

To no avail, Papa continued to insist on my sister's return.

"Tahir will bring her back soon."

This was the temporary division of offspring carried out by my mother. I was the only one who wanted to be one of the relocated children handed off. But I was too useful for her to give me away.

From then on, nothing else affected my father—unemployment, unpaid rent, a wife trying to obtain repudiation at any price since divorce was an unknown institution! Nothing else could affect him.

Some time later, I began to wet the bed. I couldn't make myself go out alone at night because I was too afraid of the dark. And then, I didn't dare wake up Mama. She simply reacted the next morning after washing me. She would give me a hard time by touching my wet body with electric wires. Afterward, I had to wash the room and my clothes. In the evening, she gave me a mat to sleep on.

"That's easier to wash and dry."

I stretched out on the ground.

When Papa sent me to spend a few vacation days with relatives in Thiès, everything was fine once more. But, the problem began again when I returned. Mama thought I was doing it on purpose, to exasperate her.

In order to comfort me, Papa told me the story that is recounted to Peul children: While a child was sleeping, Hare made him think that he was really in the toilet and could let himself go. As soon as the child began to relieve himself, Hare burst out laughing.

"I got you, I got you . . . you're in your bed," which would wake up the child.

"You see, it wasn't your fault. It's the fault of Hare, who tricked you. He's very clever, you know."

Hare's ruse was confirmed for me, because as soon as I left that place, leaving him behind, he never fooled me again.

With the birth of another child, my brother and sister came home temporarily. Space was all the more restricted. In any case, we were ordered to vacate for nonpayment of rent. But where could we go? We stayed there.

Finally, Papa found a shop in Grandak. I was the only one to learn about it. I immediately became important: I had a secret to share with my father. And we were finally going to move out . . . I began dreaming, like my mother, about a room for me alone. I began dreaming of space . . .

I asked my father if I could continue going to school.

"Of course."

I was happy. I would continue seeing my friends. I jumped with joy, and I was impatient to tell them the news, for we had been sad at the idea of possibly being separated.

Mama suggested that my father leave us in a room she had found until the summer vacation. Papa agreed.

We moved into a bare room. No shower, no toilet. And then, fleas, bugs, and rats kept watch.

Mama must have been the only one satisfied with this move—one more stage in the process of her separation from father. Curiously, in spite of her stubbornness, the number of children kept growing. And she was determined to carry out her decision, even though she was pregnant once more and almost at term.

My father came to sleep there and would leave early for Grandak. Mama didn't even fix breakfast for us any more. Papa was the one who usually did that for us, besides. Mama would still be asleep when my brother and I left for school-with empty stomachs. At noon, if she happened to be there, she rarely gave us anything to eat.

Papa paid a fee for us in a *tangana** so we could eat breakfast before going to school. When Mama found that out, she questioned us.

"Why don't you go live with your father? Only the youngest child would stay with me until I give birth . . ."

On his side, Papa insisted that we stay with Mama.

"You have to help her as much as possible—she's your mother; think about your studies, too—you're only a few steps from school."

---

*In Wolof, *tangana* means "it's hot." This is the word for a place where cheap breakfasts are served. Cups are old milk bottles that have been cleaned.

My plan to return to Grandak with my brother Laye was delayed by the arrival of a paternal uncle, coming from the Fuuta Jaloo. We had nicknamed him the "Savant" and "Know-It-All."

This uncle had never wanted to hear an explanation of how whatever-it-might-be worked. He would interrupt us after the first words on the pretense that we weren't even born when he had come to Dakar. We couldn't teach him a thing.

Mama had a gas range because the coal-burning oven was outdated in her view. One day, she left it on to let our Savant warm his breakfast (as usual, Mama was demonstrating her hospitality).

But Savant did not know how to put out the fire. I found him, crouching down and blowing with all his strength on the flame. Great beads of sweat showed that he had been working at this task for some time. He gave me a pleading look. My brother and I simply advised him to blow on the flame with greater force.

He obeyed docilely.

As soon as we heard my mother's voice, we went to the neighbor's to listen to what would happen. We could imagine Mama aghast to see the gas still burning and this huge, lanky man sweating profusely and blowing on the flame.

"I've never seen such a persistent flame," the Savant said by way of clarification. "I began blowing on it as soon as you left. Maybe we can manage together."

Without a word, Mama turned the control. She was in a bad mood. It was in our interest not to tease her.

This daughter of nobility from the Fuuta Jaloo knew how to use her birth to advantage; she considered herself superior to everybody; she looked down on her in-laws and even on us, her own children.

Our Savant left embarrassed.

After he left, Mama began once more telling us how it is wrong to mix goats and sheep in the same enclosure. We didn't understand a word. We would have liked to find out who was a goat and who was a sheep in this house. My brother often remembered the expression and asked me to choose between the two animals.

"I don't like either one of them."

Mama interrupted that dialogue.

"You're going to live with your father. Today, I'm leaving for good."

She looked at us for a while before finally deciding to walk out.

We went to my father's place in Grandak on foot. Hand in hand, we kept crying the whole way. We knew that we had lost our mother, that she wouldn't come back. Before getting to my father's place, we took care to dry our faces, wiping away the tears, so as not to draw attention to ourselves.

Papa didn't like tattletales. We had eyes that were not supposed to see. We were only supposed to speak when spoken to and to answer, only when asked a question, saying we didn't know, even if we really did. We were supposed to rein in our wishes and desires. We had to tame our bodies and minds. That would keep us out of trouble and earn us praise, such as "Oh! What good children!"

What Mama had said to us as she left must have been part of a taboo subject, long since relegated to the domain of things not to be discussed. We were gagged by the upbringing we had received.

When we arrived, Papa fixed us something to eat without asking any questions.

"You can replace me in the store . . . I won't be long."

He returned only at nightfall, with all the baggage. We'll never know what happened.

"Your mother left."

We had simply joined the little children, who were already with my father. Papa had gone to get the two-year-old from Tahir, who was passing through Dakar. That evening, the baby began crying without our knowing why. I couldn't calm her down. So, I imitated her—we mingled our tears for a while.

Oh, Mama, I can still see you after your countless showers during the day, getting dressed for breakfast, lunch, and dinner. After having done the cooking and before serving the food, you had to go rinse with a bucket of water in order to get rid of the odors from the meal you had prepared.

At other times, you would sit with a mirror propped between your feet to put on makeup, placing a beauty mark on your right cheek to make your light complexion stand out. In order to remove the hair from your armpits, you took ash between your thumb and index finger and then pulled out the hair with a quick motion. Then you dusted yourself with talcum, an odor I didn't particularly like. You used the same procedure to remove down from my forehead, from one temple to the other. With my head firmly caught between your legs, I had no way to escape. I had the impression I was a chicken being plucked. It was really painful.

"You have hair growing almost into your eyes. It's important to have a clear forehead."

But nature took over. Every morning, my father wet his hand and wiped my eyebrows, my forehead, and the length of my hair.

"Otherwise, we won't be able to see your face."

Mama, you had a session for taking care of each part of your body. Your feet soaked in a basin of lukewarm water, with a pumice stone to remove callouses on your heel and to make your toenails shine. You spread concoctions of shea butter and orange peel over your body. This process showed me a beautiful body, fine legs, and breasts that had never been suckled—all covered with this mixture every morning. You had the firm, slender body of a girl. You even had an extra treatment for your teeth once a week. To make them shine, you rubbed them with carbon, cleaned them, and polished them like kitchen pots. Your hair fell casually down your body, making me want to hide beneath it, to run my fingers through it, and to play hide-and-go-seek in it. I had the impression that we had always played that way. You brushed and combed your hair without ever braiding it; you wore a scarf to enhance your beautiful hair.

Later, when I was seventeen years old and saw Mama again, my most fervent desire was to sleep beside her. I told a neighbor woman, who seemed surprised by my wish.

"Why don't you tell her?"

"I don't dare ask her, and I don't think she would like it."

The neighbor spoke to Mama about it. My mother invited me to sleep in her bed. I didn't close my eyes the whole night—I was afraid of touching her and what she would think of me.

With Mama's physique, she hid her age. She constantly reinvented her birth date.

Still later, I almost "choked" in the waiting room of a Parisian doctor's office. I was living in London, and at my sister's invitation, I had come to spend a few days of vacation with Mama. I wanted to take advantage of every moment to speak with her and get to know her better. Here's what she told me.

"Do you think a woman doesn't menstruate any more when she's thirty-five years old?"

"Maybe, but it must be unusual at that age."

"Imagine, I'm in that situation. I think that the doctor will find a remedy."

"Remember that thirty-five years have passed since you were married."

It was useless to remind her of her age—nothing worked.

"I know your age better than you do since I brought you into the world."

"I beg you not to hide anything from the doctor."

In the final analysis, I still had the naïveté to think that you should tell the truth to your doctor for your health, and to your lawyer for your defense. Her turn came, and she went into the consulting room with twenty years in reserve. I don't know what she told the doctor. We didn't talk about it any more.

I told my sister about the visit to the doctor, and she had an answer.

"Mama is convinced that is her age—this is her sincere belief."

I was speechless. I wanted to walk out and leave. And I had thought I could manage a reconciliation with my mother. What she had just told me showed the abyss between us. Some pieces to my puzzle were missing, and I learned that she could not give them to me.

She still did not know who she was, what her age was, and who I was with respect to her.

Now, she states and repeats that she loved us. From a distance, maybe. But I have never felt enough warmth from her to open my heart to her. Her love must have been secret, hidden behind the toughness of her pride. Mama could not lower herself to her children's level. As far as I am concerned, if she loved me, I have never found any sign of it.

In Grandak, my father's shop took up only a tiny space. My sister and I slept on a bed squeezed under the counter. My brothers and my father on mats, spread on the floor. In Papa's opinion, no room was sufficiently secure. He liked to have us beside him. Much later, he found a room for us. We didn't stay there very much, preferring to remain piled upon one another in the shop.

Keeping shop was exhausting work, and the profits were far from ample. We saved bits of candle. Everything here was sold by the piece—nobody could afford a package of cigarettes, a package of sugar, or even an entire loaf of bread. Everything was counted, measured, weighed, and the profit margin was minimal. What my father considered his rest time was the moment when he went to stock up on cases of oil, drinks, or blocks of ice. After being broken up into chunks worth ten or twenty-five francs each, the ice was carefully wrapped and stored in a wooden ice chest to keep the drinks cool. This was our refrigerator-freezer.

"I'll only tell you about the things that bring in more profit: by the piece, a package of cigarettes is worth fifteen francs; a package of detergent, ten francs; a loaf of bread, broken up, brings ten francs; oil, sugar, milk, etc., bring twenty-five francs."

I revolted at this inventory.

"But Papa, you don't make anything, and you don't even rest. You know, I thought we were rich."

"That's a myth. Everybody thinks that since I am behind a counter with a stock of merchandise and some money in the cash register."

"That's disgusting. You know, I'm going to help you. I will build houses for you. One day, you'll see, you won't have to work any more. I'm going to do the same for all the young beggars loitering in the streets of Dakar."

"I'm sure you will do all that, but if you could just start by not giving credit to people without my knowing it, that would be good, since, while we're waiting for the castles, we run the risk of being put out in the street."

I was caught unaware. People had indeed taken advantage of my father's absence to ask me for things on credit—money they would never pay back, in fact.

"I'm going to show you the account register," my father continued. "Everyone has owed us money for quite a while. We live in the land of appearances: *Lebalma, abalma, mayma.** Valid or not, people hold out their hands, and we cannot be prosperous simply by giving charity. You know, the men send their wives or their children—they do not leave the house unless family members have not been persuasive."

Quoting each person who owed money, Papa imitated them so well that I broke out laughing. Who would have thought that this man, who lowered his eyes with humility and respect in the face of his interlocutors, was capable of observing the person and beyond that of describing or imitating the person. I understood that nothing around him escaped his notice. He began to roll his eyes, letting his lower lip stick out as he changed his voice.

"Papa Barry, would you lend me some money to go shopping—look at the children. I will pay you as soon as my husband returns."

"I can't lend money to anyone with unpaid debts. Your husband and you owe me money."

Then he waved his register of accounts.

"I can go without eating, but do it for the children. You are a Muslim, so what do you do about the charity every Muslim owes his neighbor?"

---

* "Give me credit, lend me, give me." This all means to them "give me." [Credit, loan, gift, in Peul.—*Trans.*]

Then the children begin to cry, without mentioning the mother, who keeps on more desperately.

Papa continued his explanation more seriously.

"You give more credit without ever being completely repaid. When those customers want to borrow again, they come to show their 'good intentions' by making a payment on their debts. Then they are delighted, thinking that they have taken you in. They think they are more clever than the others.

My father opened a suitcase containing a great variety of objects—cheap jewelry, clothes, women's shoes—all given as security. Men bring their watches and especially their corrective eyeglasses as a sign that their debts will be paid off without delay since it is impossible to work without glasses.

One day I ran into Mama by chance. I had not seen her since the day she announced she was leaving. Nobody knew exactly where she was, but everyone thought they knew with whom she was staying. It was a big surprise to see her carrying her baby on her back, although this is a custom for us.

I was glad to see her, but there was no sign of emotion from either of us. I would have liked to throw myself in her arms, to say something nice and tender. But I wasn't too sure what; I would have had trouble finding the words since I had never heard them. I was as motionless as a statue.

Nothing had changed.

"While the divorce I requested is pending, will you tell your father to return some of my clothes so I can carry this baby?"

Then, turning around to stop a taxi, she left without even saying good-bye.

I went back to my father's place in tears. I was upset with him for moving with Mama's luggage. I would have taken some clothes to her if I had known where I could find her. The thought of discovering where Mama was staying became an obsession for me. I wanted to see this mother, but not to stay with her. There was no question of living together, but I simply wanted to know how she was. To help her if necessary.

Apparently a shopkeeper had seen her go into one house on several occasions. He sympathized with my distress and was ready to help me.

"Will you promise me never to tell anyone that I am the one who helped you find her?"

"Yes."

"Your mother disappointed our community," he continued. "How could she, the daughter of a *wàlliyu* (a learned holy man), who is supposed to set an example of irreproachable behavior, let herself be caught in such a dishonorable situation? Did your mother think about her father, who must be turning over in his grave, about her family, and about what she is, what she represents? Being a noble is not simply a kind of behavior; it is a way of life. As for her fiancé, he's a crazy man who should be put away. How could any man marry a woman with children when he is free to ask for the hand of an unmarried girl?"

His words were making me drunk, and I would have liked to bite him, to yell at him that it wasn't important to know who Mama was with, even if it was the devil—this was my mother, and I wanted to see her. At my tender age already, I needed to learn how to negotiate and to keep my resentment hidden in order to get this information that was so important to me. Very difficult! I mustn't get carried away; I had to listen to disagreeable things without reacting. Yes, that was it.

I didn't understand the Peul. What was bothering them? I would understand later that a high birth rate took priority over everything for this proud people.

I followed my guide from Grandak to Dakar. He paid the bus fare for both of us. Once we got out, he kept a respectful distance. He did not want to point the place out to me, which according to him would have attracted people's attention. And who knows whether the wife thief, the kidnapper of mothers with children, might not be in the vicinity. He showed me a house right in the center of Dakar.

Running, I left my guide without even thanking him but found only my mother's fiancé. Without greeting him, I asked where Mama was.

"She'll be back before long."

He was cordial and immediately offered to share the dinner he was eating—a ragoût with an aroma I liked. I thanked him, letting him understand that I wasn't hungry, although my stomach was growling since my last meal had been breakfast.

Mama came back before long. Her fiancé left us alone.

"If I were in a hole, you would manage to find me, brat!"

And she began hitting me. I tried to get loose and run out,

but she held on to me firmly. I didn't cry. My perpetual calm exasperated her more and more. She was yelling; people had gathered and were begging her to stop beating me because she might kill me.

"I don't ever want to see you again—neither you nor your father, and the next time you try to find me, I'll strangle you, understand? What I regret most is that I didn't smother you when you were born. I really regret that. I should have."

She dragged me over to a *kaar** and forcibly sat me in it. She wanted the ultimate humiliation for me. I was thinking that she might have at least taken me in a taxi, which would have protected me from people's stares.

I had been savagely beaten, my clothes were torn, and people kept staring at me until she had left me in my father's hands.

"I hope you've understood, once and for all, that I don't ever want to see you again," she concluded.

She left, and my father began bandaging my wounds. Once again, he avoided asking questions.

The atmosphere was heavy. I had the impression that my younger brothers and my sister understood what had just happened without needing for me to explain. I didn't want to cry, but I burst out sobbing. The tears that were falling were not caused by my wounds, but by something deeper in me. My child's heart had suffered a serious blow. I wanted to erase from my mind what I had suffered and heard, but the images refused to go away, and the words kept ringing in my ears. The neighbors questioned me.

"How could your mother do that?"

I didn't answer. Besides, I didn't know why. I felt that I was at a turning point, but without knowing what it meant. I was becoming someone different—my childhood and carefree existence were finished. Or perhaps just dormant.

*A pickup truck used as a collective taxi.

My first reaction was to ask Papa to cancel our meal plan and to give me the money so I could buy some cooking utensils. We had trouble eating the food they served us. We usually put vinegar in it to make the pill go down. Papa ate only after we were full.

I began to prepare meals, but only in the evening when I returned from school. I wasn't going to do better than our old cook. But this was the first act in a difficult job, the apprenticeship of adult life. At ten and one-half years old, I no longer had the same concerns as girls my age. While they were helping their mothers, I was replacing mine completely. I had trouble finding the right amount of rice and water. The rice became pasty or even a kind of porridge, although it was a staple in this country.

Papa did not blame my lack of experience, but rather the quality of the rice.

"This rice is full of starch—it's not your fault at all."

He ate and encouraged the others to do the same.

Some evenings, he closed the shop earlier than usual so he could tell us stories, which were sometimes replaced with sessions of acrobatics. Papa would begin walking around the store on his hands—my brothers followed him, and it was a challenge to see who could hold out the longest. As a variation, he would do push-ups and all sorts of exercise, just as he did with the soldiers when we lived in Rebeus: he would have liked a military career.

My sister and I really enjoyed watching these exploits. We asked for more. Each one of us tried to relieve the tension.

These premature responsibilities didn't leave me much time for school. My grades suffered. So long prizes! (What Papa liked best was my award for "good behavior," which he mentioned often to everyone except me: that might have pushed me toward "bad behavior . . .")

Balla, my uncle and my friend, helped me a lot that year. He had moved to come live near the school. He saved me long trips back and forth to Grandak by bringing me lunch. He ate at his work place; then he came to keep me company and took me back to school on his Mobylette so I didn't have to walk. Some evenings, he took me back to Grandak. I was quite moved by his concern. I have never been able to thank him or to tell him how much I loved him (you don't say that, and I was to lose him years later without having confided this to him). He went out of the way to make me happy and helped me not to suffer too much from the separation of our parents.

To go to school each morning, I placed my brother on my lap even though he had become pretty heavy. This kept us from paying an extra fare in the express bus, although Papa was paying for both of us. He got off two stops after me and kept the change. Only a favored child was welcomed for lunch at our mother's place; but she wasn't there very often. My brother went begging for food or simply spent the return fare he usually had with him. This meant that we often returned to Grandak on foot or by hitchhiking, when I could find him at his school. We would stop at a crossroads, and when the light turned red, he would go up to a driver and tell him we were orphans, hoping to get sympathy. When the driver was moved, he would pick us up. Did the driver believe it or was he just pretending? No matter, the comedy always worked.

This game ended one day when my father found out about

it in an innocuous way. I had confiscated my brother's school materials, demanding that he return the bus fare to me—and he had spent it as usual. My brother felt that he didn't owe me anything, since I could get home free by hitchhiking, thanks to "his services." This meant that he came out the winner in all respects. Wanting to know what the argument was all about, Papa discovered that his son was hungry and was playing hooky, and that we were coming home by hitchhiking.

A school was found for him close to my father's shop, which did him a lot of good. But it was true that he began stuttering and losing his self-assurance. His stuttering did not amuse us for very long.

Papa took advantage of the Easter vacation to have my brothers circumcised. But I was irritated to hear father talking to them and telling them that now they would be men, so I wanted to see what earned them that status all of a sudden.

Had they achieved it by the simple fact of circumcision? Apparently so.

Curiosity made me look for confirmation. I didn't want to be caught in the act, so I took advantage of father's absence to check with my youngest brother, who was going to be four years old, and I asked him not to tell anyone. I saw a white bandage spotted with red around the end of his penis. I was really embarrassed by my curiosity, because I knew I had just broken a taboo.

At the same time, I wouldn't have attributed any importance to this transgression if there hadn't been so much work to be done. Not one of my brothers was supposed to do any work before they were completely healed. I didn't have any help—I had to do everything by myself. And what's more, my work was not recognized as work: it was just one of those things taken for granted. I never heard the word "thank you," which I love and really liked to hear. In the evening, when I was dead tired, I had to be present for their daily *kasag** during the entire period of their convalescence. They would begin wiggling in their flowing *njulli* robe,† wearing no underwear and with their circumcision staff in one hand. The others would join in, and the saraband would continue late into the night.

I kept getting up early, at the same time as my father, in

*The songs and dances of the evening circumcision ceremonies.
†A circumcised person.

order to get as much done as possible. Mornings were calm and cool.

Mama often came to bring food for my brothers. This did not keep me from having to cook because I no longer ate what she prepared. I went about my business, ignoring her. When she spoke to me, I didn't answer. I was only keeping the "reserved attitude" that she had told me to keep. What she had said to me the day when I went looking for her still echoed in my ears, like the refrain of some haunting canticle. My aunts, who came with her, cried with sorrow.

Once they had healed, my brothers could dress like everyone else, and their *njulli* robes were thrown out. I thought I could have some help with the domestic chores then, but Laye talked to me about the women's work that he would not have to do any longer: he had become a man. Since the other two were too young, they helped me more or less. They did not have the advantage of status.

Everyone thought it was fine that I devote myself to my brothers and sister. I was considered an adult, a responsible person. I behaved that way—so I didn't have any right to change. But I was outraged by Laye's attitude: either everyone works or I stop—whatever might happen!

I was convinced that I was born free, not holding a pot in one hand and a broom in the other. The clashes had begun, and I protested against my brother's status as a man excluding him from any work considered feminine.

My paternal uncles had all come from their village in the Fuuta Jaloo to attend the ceremony of my brothers' rites of passage. They showed a marked favoritism for my brother Laye, because he was a boy. They didn't find me very pleasant because I didn't say much. At times, I didn't say anything at all. According to them, you have to beware of people like me. They no longer even used my name, but preferred to use the term *ndjudu*, an expression of their contempt.

One of the reasons my uncles gave to justify their criticism was that I had never been able to use the polite Peul "you," which is *ɓe*. I didn't do much better in other respects: I would look them in the eye when I spoke to them; I didn't hold my bowl when I was eating (which is a sign of a poor upbringing); I cooked Senegalese dishes without taking into account their revulsion to *gejj** and *yéet*,† which had a strong odor but an agreeable taste in *ceeb*. For me, you have to cook the way the people who live there do it. If my uncles did not understand that, they could simply go home and be happy to drink milk, their staple food.

Besides everything else, it seemed scandalous to them for a girl to go to school—a sacrilege, a mortal sin. In short, nothing about me was to their liking.

My uncles used my brother to get even with me. They never laid a hand on us since, inwardly, they knew I wouldn't take it. When I fought with my brother, my uncles and my father yelled at him like trainers in a boxing ring.

"You're the man, don't let yourself be dominated by a person who is only a weak woman."

But a fight's a fight, not a frame of mind. They held it against me anyway that I didn't consider my age: I was older, so I was stronger. Their protégé—their man, was often beaten, in the ring as well as in the classroom. I took it out on him without letting myself go completely—just enough to maintain my mastery over him.

I must have dissidence in my genes.

Before he reached his "manly status," my brother and I liked each other fine. We went to the *làmb*,‡ sneaked into the stadium to watch soccer games—my scraped knees paid the price. We often had memories in common, and he was my friend; when a boy wanted to take me on, Laye came to my defense. He had always felt he was my protector.

On the other hand, I got burned cooking for him; I washed and ironed his clothes. I was a real mother for him and the others.

So, since no one was grateful, I decided to go on strike for two weeks.

*A type of dried fish.
†A sea mollusk. [Cymbium, a genus of marine snails.—*Trans.*]
‡Fight games (or, the stadium).

Determined not to touch a simple piece of candy in Papa's shop, I went to the market that day to buy some fruit for myself with my own money! My uncles and my father were surprised and asked me the same questions.

"Are you sick?"

"Why? I'm fine," I answered.

"You didn't eat your breakfast, and here's your little sister waiting for you to wash her."

"That's not my job."

So my father did the task.

"It's getting late, and you haven't gone to the market?"

"Yes, I did! I've just come back," and I showed them the fruit I had bought for myself. "Besides, I think it's beginning to get hot."

"Did I hear you right? You're not serious," said my father.

Without answering, I went to stretch out beneath some trees, with my fruit, some books—more than I was going to read. I was disturbed constantly.

"At least, you're going to prepare lunch?"

"No!"

"Tell us what's wrong."

"Everything is fine, but since I am just a woman, I have no desire to do anything at all."

"Come on, you have to help us."

"I won't work alone."

"You know that you work better than we do. We'll work all that out, but you can't suddenly leave me alone with your brothers and your sister. You've always been the mother and me the father."

I remained inflexible. At noon, Papa left to buy something to eat for the children; he did the same thing for dinner.

That evening, I went to a *làmb,* which I hadn't done for a long time. The amateur wrestlers were going to face off to the sound of a tam-tam that night at Le Bayal, the arena in Grandak. It was free, and even before the wrestlers appeared, there was a real excitement in the air. Laye and the other boys were scuffling with each other, imitating professional fighters.

They were chased from the arena before the arrival of the combatants, who were cheered by all the spectators. The tam-tam sounded more loudly than ever. Sweating and with a smile, the fighters entered, remembering their past exploits and wearing their *ngemb** pulled tight around their waists with strings of gris-gris. They looked like fine statues, covered with shea oil that made their muscles stand out and allowed them to slip out of the grip of their opponents at the same time. They gave off an odor of wild animals.

The next morning, the strike continued. Over the following days, father and the children went between canned sardines, buttered bread with chocolate, and warm milk to fill their stomachs. Papa even boiled some *ñàmbi*† as a change from the eggs they wouldn't eat.

As for me, I stayed on my diet of varied fruit.

My uncles threatened me with retaliation and physical punishment that would bring me back to reason and a better disposition, they thought. Papa tried unsuccessfully to touch my sensibility by sending my little sister crying for food. He had to be unaware of my determination once I had decided that things would not get to me. Just as when I decided that Mama would never hear me cry any more when she beat me. What she was striking was no longer my body. I had suppressed all sensation.

Uncle Balla, the only one who could usually get me to change my mind or coax me out of my silence, came to negotiate. Papa and the other uncles were counting on his mediation. I didn't listen to him.

I said to myself, "It's a pity, really disturbing, to see these adults totally dependent on a person they consider to be inferior."

After three days of rest and pouting, things suddenly fell back into place, as if by magic. I had only to utter a wish, and it was instantly fulfilled by these "supermen" who anticipated

*A type of cache-sexe.
†Manioc.

my desires and toed the line from then on. In spite of that, I was sorry that I had not used this procedure earlier. I hadn't thought of its effectiveness. The results were beneficial for everybody.

The silent treatment became my weapon. I could use it against anyone. It wasn't difficult for me. I could remain around people for an indefinite period without speaking to them and pass them without even noticing the color of their clothes. This was neither hostility nor animosity, nor even rancor. I simply willed to ignore their presence.

Father had attempted in vain to use religion to teach me a lesson—"You mustn't sulk, you mustn't refuse to eat. God does not like that"—but I didn't see anything bad about it. This was my way of maintaining my distance and protecting myself. I could easily become detached from things and people. Things interested me only when I was trying to conquer them; afterward, they no longer interested me. It was that way for a long time and even with my prizes at school.

Another way for me to maintain a distance was go to the point of imagining anyone who bothered me with an animal's head or with a body part alienated from its proper function—an eye that spoke, for example. I was really frustrated not to know how to draw so I could draw all the images jostling around in my child's head.

Mama got several people to intervene in order to get me to go see her.

It was no use telling my father that I was not angry with mother. He insisted.

"Not speaking to her is a way of being angry—you shouldn't do that."

How could I explain to him that Mama no longer existed for me?

I could never conceive how a hand that has caressed you, wiped away your tears, reassured you, comforted . . . could hurt you.

Father and his friends repeated, "A mother is the one who gave you life. You must do everything to satisfy her."

As an example, they told me about the fight between the stone and the egg, the Peul version of "Le Pot de Terre et le Pot de Fer."* I was supposedly the egg and my mother, obviously, the stone. Whether I bumped against the stone or the stone bumped against me, the result was the same: I always ended up broken.

To top it off, they demanded that I go to beg her pardon! I could not understand. This injustice made me cry out. How could you beg the pardon of somebody, whoever it might be, to whom you had never done a thing, somebody who had savagely beaten you, given you an order never to go looking for her again, and who even regretted not having smothered you when you were born?

I wondered how my own father could so easily forgive everybody and forget the outrages he had suffered. By dint of being

* "Le Pot de Terre et le Pot de Fer" ("The Earthen Pot and the Iron Pot"), La Fontaine, *Fables*, Book V, ii.—*Trans.*

constantly besieged by the preachers of forgiving offenses, who irritated me to the greatest degree, I finally accepted going to see her and, in particular, speaking to her. I was accompanied by my father and one of his friends and had expressed my conditions to both of them.

"I have no excuses to offer and, all the more, I won't kneel to make them. I am going simply to satisfy you and not in my own interest, as you put it."

They accepted, while thinking that, once I was in front of my mother, they could get me to change my mind.

We went one evening. Mama began to cry, just like the aunts who were also there. They even managed to bring tears to my eyes. Mama wanted me to spend the night with her. That was too much for me. I left with my father. All of them thought that peace had been restored.

Is it possible to erase a long-standing pain that has left persistent traces in the head and the heart?

The divorce proceedings were going along. There had been several hearings at which the presence of my brothers, my sister, and myself was required. It was painful to witness these revelations, which we would gladly have avoided. Mama had her witnesses who stubbornly insisted on things they knew nothing about. They claimed to have kinship ties with her. There were two of them: a tall gentleman who had been my maternal grandfather's *taalibe** and who felt obliged to defend Mama against everybody; the other one was Tahir, the woman who had taken advantage of the windfall offered to take my little sister at the moment when Mama had scattered her children around. By agreement with my mother, she claimed to be her sister.

The chief justice of the court asked me what kinship there was linking this woman to Mama. I wasn't unaware that I had a number of uncles and aunts or that my maternal grandfather had had sixteen wives, but I was certain that Tahir had absolutely no kinship with mother.

"They are friends," I answered.

Mama and her supposed relatives were very upset with me. I didn't understand since I had simply told the truth, as I had been instructed to do by the bar. But with such divergent interests at stake, it was necessary to feel somehow at fault, no matter to which party one turned. For my mother, I had taken sides, when in fact I didn't have one. As a result, this affected the "reconciliation" that had been conceived between us.

Then it was the last day of this trial by humiliation. Papa also had two witnesses: the landlords of the shop and of the house where we were living confirmed that he was in fact liv-

*A religious disciple.

ing with us. We were all on edge but relieved at the same time, since we thought that we had nothing more to do with the justice system.

We were definitively placed under father's guardianship. But he had to pay child support to mother, who had the two youngest children.

Before leaving the hearing room, Papa put his cap back on. An overzealous gendarme told him to take it off and, without giving him time to do so, snatched it from his head. Papa reacted with a blow. He was immediately arrested, placed in a Jeep, and taken to the National Gendarmerie. Laye held on to the vehicle. He didn't want to let our father go. The car stopped, and the gendarmes around him made him get in with them.

I was calm—I was carrying my little sister on my back without a pagne to tie her there, and she was holding on for dear life; I was holding my two brothers by the hand. We took the bus in front of the court house in order to go find Papa and my brother. In tears, Mama had also joined us.

The gendarmes kept away the witnesses and the curious onlookers who had followed us just to have something sensational to tell their families. In any case, we had been objects of annoying curiosity all day long. This had begun when I appeared on the witness stand. We were beginning to get used to this unhealthy game.

"You are going to leave with your mother—we have to retain your father for some formalities, and we will release him right after."

"We don't want to leave with our mother—the court appointed our father as guardian," I said.

"You don't want to stay with your own mother?"

They stressed this question, which had no effect on us. Mama was forced to leave alone. The gendarmes offered us something to eat while their colleagues took Papa's fingerprints. He was not subjected to the humiliation of wearing handcuffs. I was grateful to them for this.

They were proper enough to wait for us to leave before interrogating him.

We were hungry, but we all refused to eat, even our little sister, who was only three years old. I was proud of her. As the chief of these "commandos," I was almost eleven years old, and Laye was nine. We were not heroes, but rather a bunch of poor kids who wanted them either to release our father or keep us with him.

We didn't see anything serious in what Papa had done. He was exasperated, that's all. Why all this circus because of a blow? If they had to arrest everyone who hit somebody, there wouldn't be enough prisons.

You only had to walk around Dakar a bit to see fights.

We could be father's best lawyers. We found nothing but attenuating circumstances for him. No person, strong or weak, whoever it may be, can accept being humiliated in front of his wife and children without reacting. He had certainly reacted because he was desperate. Up to that day, he had thought Mama would return home.

Father was a calm man. It's always terrible to see the reaction of a person calm by nature. If I could only tell them . . . But they didn't ask me anything, and since I had been raised not to speak until spoken to, I didn't say anything. I had confidence in the justice system. They would release him after some formalities, as they promised. And if we could just wait for those formalities?

The gendarmes thought they could convince us by taking us to our mother's place against our will. In spite of their entreaties, we refused to get out of the car. We had decided to make them run around Dakar if necessary so they would give our father back to us. They consulted with each other.

"We can't leave these children alone in Grandak. We have to leave them under the protection of an adult."

We felt they were close to us. My little sister was being cuddled by the men in blue, whom I might have detested since they were keeping my father away from me, but I didn't dislike them. I had no more defensive or offensive reflexes.

They asked us whether we had a relative we could stay with. We told them about Uncle Balla, who, as we knew, was not home during the day, and we counted on that to get them to take us back to our father.

When the police car arrived, the gawkers gathered around; the gendarmes had to use their elbows to let us get out of the car. We hadn't foreseen that they could leave us with the neighbor lady next door to my uncle. That's what they did.

Everyone was eager to ask us questions that none of us answered. This was our group reaction, although we had not said anything to each other.

We were the stars of a sad story. The day had been long and filled with challenges—our stomachs were empty and growling. But I hated that air of pity that people put on, the horrible commiseration that places you in a position of inferiority.

At six o'clock in the afternoon, our uncle found us in front of his door since we had refused to go into the neighbor lady's house. He saw himself blessed all of a sudden with five children. He went out to buy something for us to eat. I briefly told him what had happened. He reacted with despairing gestures. The situation must be serious to put him in such a state—and I had always seen him remain self-possessed. Late that night, in order to avoid inopportune and curious people, he took us to our father's shop so we would be out of sight.

The next morning, before going to work, he told us not to say anything. We had understood that!

"Don't accept any merchandise and tell everybody that your father had to go away. You and your brother will go to school, and the other children will stay with the neighbor woman. I am going to speak with her."

In spite of my uncle's recommendations, I talked to the suppliers at six a.m. I negotiated with them in order to make some money until father would be released. I did the cooking, and my brothers helped. Laye had become the father, and he took his role quite seriously. We must have been the youngest parents in the world. Everyone asked us questions, without getting an answer. They all distorted the story in their own way: "What great children! What an unworthy mother!" And the comments continued along that line.

Fortunately, Mama didn't live in that neighborhood or nearby, and she did not come to see us. People called her all sorts of names: "child abandoner!"—"jailer!" These were insults I would like to erase from my memory. People's passion made them forget that, whatever she might have done, this was our mother they were treating that way.

The neighbors had completely adopted us. They brought us things to eat, washed our clothes, and gave me enough practical advice to become a cordon bleu chef. They missed my father for several reasons. To mention only the financial side, he gave them credit, while that word was banished, stricken from my vocabulary. They all wanted to visit him. They came around to offer to keep my sister or my younger brothers. I thanked them for their kindness, which I perhaps mistakenly distrusted—and I gave the pretext that we wanted to remain together. In fact, we were comforted to be together and unified among ourselves. I felt that we could be independent, autonomous, by refusing adult help, which could not be without some payback.

The shop, run by children, drew a great number of people. I had decided to fill it with merchandise, which gave me the illusions that everything was going well. The suppliers made their deliveries free of charge. That was their support.

My uncle came to see us every evening and helped us to close up toward midnight and to count the money. I began to keep accounts and to pay the suppliers on time. Uncle Balla had given up trying to reason with me.

"You shouldn't be in business, you should go to school and leave the little ones with the neighbors."

He was wasting his breath. There was no way I would leave the children alone.

I had decided to replace my father, to take care of my brothers and sister as long as he might be in prison.

I took Bouba to be vaccinated before he started school. The days passed without my father being released; my uncle brought us his news. Uncle was our only support and our only messenger.

"Tomorrow, I'll go to the prison to see your father. He is at 'Cent Mètres Carrés.'* According to his lawyer, he will be released soon. He will be given a suspended sentence."

I didn't understand what my uncle was talking about. He had explained to me what "suspended sentence" meant. As for the lawyers, I had seen some of them at court. I had been very impressed by their black robes and their white plastrons.

"I'll go with you next time, right?"

"They don't admit children to the prison."

"Yes, I'm going with you. And if you don't take me there, we'll all go together on our own."

He thought it over. He knew what I was capable of doing. All that interested me was to see my father. I didn't want to hear talk about rules or permission to be solicited!

My uncle gave in.

Our meeting was set for two o'clock in front of the Roxy Cinema, next to my school.

The next day, Laye and I got up as usual to meet the suppliers. One day like the rest since father's arrest. We ate a little early. Laye was going to replace me in the store and stay with the children.

I dressed up for Papa. I was at the meeting place ahead of time. When my uncle got there, he whistled.

"Mademoiselle, I don't recognize you . . . , is that really you?"

* "One Hundred Square Metres."—*Trans.*

I wasn't in a mood for jokes. I was nervous and tense.

I had no idea what a prison might be like. I imagined the worst and could see my father in a situation of indescribable suffering.

My uncle hugged me tightly—we had the same painful impression. I burst into tears.

"You know, you're a big, brave girl. You have to promise me not to cry when you see your father. Everything will be all right. We won't go until I have your promise to keep smiling."

I struggled to put on a smile, a very timid one. After I dried my tears, he had me turn around so he could admire my pretty dress, which chased away my frown.

We arrived in front of a huge building surrounded with barbed wire. My uncle went in by a side door and showed a paper to the guards. I waited for him in the courtyard. We went toward a cell block. There were too many men behind the grills and also a lot of visitors—all speaking in a loud voice. I looked for my father without managing to see him. My uncle lifted me up. Then I saw him. He had lost weight. He came close. I didn't want to speak. I managed to poke my little fingers through the grate to touch his.

My uncle and father talked about me, about us, in a coded language, and in Peul, besides. I couldn't understand everything they were saying.

Papa asked me: "Are the children doing all right and are you working at school? I hope so."

My uncle quickly replied, "Oh, yes, yes."

"Don't worry, I'll be back with you soon."

There was a buzzer to announce the end of the visiting hour. I pulled my fingers back. That contact had made me feel so good! I went back to run my father's shop with confidence. As for my brothers' questions, they showed more curiosity than uneasiness.

"He's doing well, and he will be released soon," I repeated to them.

Papa still remained in prison for some time. He came one evening, knocking at the shop door. I didn't know how much time he had spent in prison, but it had seemed like an eternity. We wanted him to tell us what had happened there, as if he were telling a new fable. "Once upon a time . . ."

He avoided questions, blessing us and telling us how proud of us he was.

Uncle Balla and my father are discussing our future. They have agreed that no decision will be made before the summer vacation, giving us time to finish the school year. Listening to them, we suspect something important is going to take place, but we're not too sure what. Anyway, we don't think we can be more upset than we have already been. Too many unexpected events have taken place in a short time.

Time slips away relentlessly. I keep doing the same chores, always at the same time.

I began to worry as soon as I was happy. Fear, nervousness, doubts paralyzed me. I felt that something unknown was going to happen to me. That is why I wanted to know what the future had in store for me, but there was nothing to enlighten me.

Finally, the school year began again; but instead of going into the second year of the intermediate level, I was sent to a special class for girls who did not have a high enough average to continue in the classical program. I was good enough not to have to repeat a year, but not good enough to be accepted in the normal class.

Our program was distinctive for its sewing and child care courses that we attended every Wednesday evening. The school made of you a good housekeeper in case you did not succeed in your studies. What my teacher and the principal surely did not know was that I had not waited for this training to become a good housekeeper and, still better, the mother of a family. I wanted to scream and remind them of my earlier grades, when I was one of the best pupils in the selective program, in spite of my numerous household and family concerns.

Since we had moved, school was the only place where I could see my friends, especially Kine and Sarah. I had promised them that I would get my Certificat d'Études Primaires [certificate of primary study] so I could join them at the lycée the following year. We did not want to go either to the Blaise Diagne Lycée or the Van Vollenhoven Lycée, which were mixed, but rather to the Kennedy Lycée, which had a magical ring to it that had become familiar to me. I would catch myself sounding it out letter by letter. I had planned to meet my pals the following year. I knew that I did well in school without any great effort—I learned without any problem and remembered easily. I was going to start working more seriously. My problem was not academic.

In the meanwhile, I would go to play with my friends during recess; there was only a door separating the two classes. I couldn't stand to be separated from them or to make new friends in my class. For a person who thought she was indifferent to many things, I must have unwittingly been faithful in friendship and firm in my convictions.

In spite of our almost non-existent relationship, Mama "stopped me" one day as I was passing in front of her workplace. This was the only road I could take. I would have liked to find a different one.

"I need to talk to you. You're going to stop being a child and listen to me, all right?"

She was holding on to me so I had no choice. She took me into an office where there was another woman that she introduced as her superior.

"Is she the one this is all about?" the woman asked.

"Yes, I need to talk to her, and I'd like for you to stay with us."

"Yes, of course; I'm a mother and I know how it is."

"When I left your father, my brothers disowned me, and they even refused to take me in. They thought I should return to my husband. I ought to have been under his guardianship since I had left theirs and that of my father. I divorced against their advice—they could not stand this disobedience from me. I would have liked to give you a different image of myself rather than that of a woman living outside of marriage. It is painful to recognize that the man you married is unable to fulfill his duties after you married him against the advice of your parents. That means you can't complain to anyone. You left your social milieu, your family, and your country for him, and you gave him your youth. Was I supposed to stay in the street with no roof, think that my father's *barki** would protect me? I work in this maternal and child shelter where I give knitting and embroidery lessons to young women, which allows me to be financially independent, as I always have been, even with your

*Benediction.

father. I am living alone and raising your two brothers. Your father has never given us a food allowance, and because of you, I'm not sending the bailiffs after him (which she ended up doing, nevertheless, but there was nothing to be seized!). Knowing when you leave, I managed to be behind the window to see you go by. I knew that if I called you, you wouldn't come. Every parent's desire is to see their children succeed better in every way than oneself. You have to succeed. A good diploma and a good job, these are the real husband for a woman, do you understand? As for my behavior, society condemns me because I am not in the institution of marriage in which one is supposed to live and die even when you don't like it. My family tells me that I am dragging their name through mud and shame. So I've lost you, my children, when you are my only success. I don't have to explain or justify myself; time will help you understand better, and I hope it won't be at your own expense."

"You are very proud. That's fine. You get that from me, at least, and you make up your own mind, I don't doubt it at all. Understand that you can't show your pride unless you are your own person and independent. You cannot hold out your hand and maintain your pride—these are incompatible."

"Finally, I ask you to get help with your studies. Do it for yourself, not for me."

She wrote down the address of a girl who would see me every Thursday to give me tutoring lessons.

I left her without a word—neither for her nor for the other woman, who was satisfied just to let out prolonged sighs.

I had just spent two months in my new class. I was doing my best to apply myself in all subjects. I dreamed of being in the lycée with my friends, and that made me happy. I could already see myself in uniform.

A short time later, I found my father in front of the principal's office at my old school. I asked him what he was doing there.

"I've come to get your certificate of attendance. We are going to have to return to Guinea."

This answer crushed me. I ran to class, trying to hold back the tears that were flooding down my face.

"What's the matter?" the teacher asked.

"I'm sick and I'd like permission to go home."

He sent for the monitor to take me to the school infirmary. Confronted with my insistence that I wanted to go home and my tears, he finally gave in and wished for me to get well quickly.

When I got back to Grandak, Papa had already gotten home. He avoided asking me questions, although I was supposed to be in school. This silence was better. I went back into my favorite position, sitting with my chin on my knees and my arms held at my side. My whole past life was flashing through my head. I couldn't suppress the images—they stuck defiantly in my mind. Every scratch, every mark, every instant represented a state of being, a situation. I had the impression that, for each phase of my life, I had to draw up a balance sheet before anything else hit me. I let my tears flow without saying a thing, without a sigh, in the most absolute silence.

I could stay in that fetal position for hours. People would leave me alone then. I ended up with violent headaches. And my sight was affected.

Seeing me in that state set my father beside himself. He told anyone who went by that he didn't know what he had done to the Good Lord to have a mute child (me), a stutterer (Laye), and a "thorny-ass" (my brother Bouba, who was ruining him—he never came home without his trousers being ripped at the knees and the behind, and his shirt at the elbows).

"You have to be the most miserable of the unfortunate to sit like that. Only an orphan with no father or mother could stay all curled up like you right now."

"I am an orphan, don't you think?"

"I got a divorce from your mother, and the load is becoming too heavy for me as it is for you. You're getting skinnier in front of my eyes . . . It's difficult for you to be the youngest mama in the world, as it is for me to be the "father-hen." In Guinea, your grandmother and your aunt that you don't even know will be happy to help me raise you."

"What about my studies?"

He avoided the topic.

"Put your things in a suitcase—you'll stay with your Uncle Balla, your friend, so you can finish the studies you're so fond of."

Why had he gone after my certificate of attendance? That seemed strange to me, that's all.

I understood that, to get me to move, Papa was promising me anything.

All the same, I had a glimmer of hope for my studies, although my parents had taken everything away from me: my childhood and now my education. How far would they go?

Until the day for the departure, Papa kept reassuring me: only my brothers and sister would leave for Guinea. I would go to see them during the summer vacation. I was sad to see them leave; for the first time, I would be separated from all of them. I hugged them to me. My sister gave me a big smile.

The trucks were overloaded with baggage. The weight limit had already been exceeded even before the passengers got on, and Guinean roads had a reputation for the fatal accidents they caused. Travelers did not seem to worry. Couples were separated, but children remained with their mothers.

I was getting worried with these huge, overloaded trucks.

"You're going to have to hold on to keep from falling."

I had lain down on a mat beside the truck with the children, waiting for the departure, set for midnight. Then I heard my father and Uncle Balla.

"You see, we won't have to chase her to get her on. Luckily, she's sleeping."

I got up suddenly. I took off running. Everyone who was there ran after me, and they finally caught me. They put me in the truck, which started without any delay. Papa held me in his arms; I pushed him away. My father had tricked me; he had betrayed my trust.

My uncle, my friend, was an accomplice to my misfortune. What was the worth of all the efforts he had put forth taking care of me for over a year? I was crushed by this betrayal. Now that I think back, there would be others alleged to be in my interest.

I was determined to jump out of the truck while it was moving. Die or be free.

Papa held me, caressing my hair. He thought he could get off more easily with this method of calming me and putting me to sleep, which had always worked up to this moment.

"Cry," he said. "It's certain that you won't cry all the way to Guinea."

I went to sleep. I didn't wake up before Kaolack the next morning.

Everybody got off the trucks to rest. The next departure took place at night.

Papa wanted to help us clean up. I refused to let him help me pour the water from a fairly heavy can: I did it alone, just like a big person. I even refused to eat breakfast or to drink from the cans he had filled with fresh water in Dakar to keep us from having to drink the undrinkable salty water in Kaolack. I had definitely stopped talking. Papa didn't leave me alone, and when he did, I was left in the hands of hefty fellows who were to keep an eye on me.

In the evening, crushed under their own weight, the trucks went back on the road. We had left the paved section of Senegal and started off on the rough roads of Guinea. When we came to make-shift bridges or steep hills, we had to get off so the truck could make it. We were shaken and bumped like pieces of popcorn. People held on wherever they could—the sides of the truck, the steel bars separating us from the driver for the people close to the cabin, and overhead bars for the taller people. Our behinds were bruised, not to speak of baggage falling on top of us. The people who were used to the road would, according to the truck's movements, lift their behinds off the baggage where they were sitting to soften the shocks. They ended up hitting their heads against the iron bars or the buckets attached to them. Then they had a hard fall. Watching them, I understood with desperation that you couldn't foresee the nature of the shock—that it was better to hold on where you were, or where you could. Otherwise, it wasn't possible to save head or behind.

Some pregnant women, close to term, were very bitter—they would ask if you couldn't be careful when you fell and would accuse you of stepping on their toes. They would vomit, and it was painful to watch them; there was fear that a miscarriage might be awaiting them. For financial reasons, their husbands wanted to see them give birth in their village rather than in Dakar.

We were on the women's truck—Papa was the only man allowed, because of us no doubt. There was a lot of chatter and only the shocks made the talkative women shut up. Our passing raised a trail of dust that we had to swallow. We drowned in it. Not even our eyebrows were spared. The colors of our clothes disappeared under a reddish coat that I had seen for the first time in Casamance.

We looked like phantoms, we were becoming the termite hills you see in the bush. Laye was laughing until he cried looking at the others, but he couldn't see himself! The truck traveled all night. We stopped at cheap "joints" where hygiene was not a priority; Papa would get out the ever-present canned sardines, with an odor that still makes me uneasy today.

As we went on, I withdrew from my father. Didn't eat, didn't speak to him. I kept hoping that hunger would bring me the death that I desired so much. It didn't work. My desire for suicide was only on hold, blurred, almost invisible, but I didn't want to give in. Each time I was obliged to do something, the desire to end my life came back. I had always seen myself in that situation. I could remember a man who committed suicide by jumping off the great mosque in Dakar; I envied him and thought I would do as he did one day, to end it all.

During those lugubrious hours when I thought I didn't care about life any longer, something happened to prevent me from "going through with it," but for how long?

My little brother, Mam, who was almost five years old, took advantage of people's lack of attention to play with the other children at getting on and off the trucks. He fell. His cries woke everybody—the people who had just washed in order to look more human, the people dozing off in the shade of a tree to rest from the trip that was only beginning. Instinctively, I recognized the voice of a bleeding person, like a mother in the middle of the savannah who senses her child in danger. I ran quickly to pick him up and carry him on my back.

"Those poor kids, living alone with their father. How can a man take care of children? Their mother abandoned them. Even a hen sits on her eggs . . . So, all the more reason . . ."

These spiteful words disgusted me. At the same time, they made me want to live and protect my children.

I stayed with Mam all the time, washed him, and gave him water to drink from the river using a large tree leaf.

Father and the others joined me. I was going to eat and watch over my "little ones" like a mother lion.

We got back on the truck for another departure. I marveled at the beautiful, verdant landscape in silence. Tall termite hills, ochre earth, mountains, valleys, *boowe*,* golden hills, waterfalls, rampant grass, wild flowers, bushes . . . This was beauty incarnate. Every day, even more picturesque landscapes appeared before my eyes. I love beauty, whatever speaks to the imagination and the soul.

I was only putting off the deadline for my own death. This was a friend who was waiting for me and who would give me relief when I turned to her. The idea of this rendezvous filled me with delight.

Papa had always told me that children go to paradise. Without knowing it, he was taking me in that direction.

*Grasslands.

We had left Dakar one Saturday at midnight without a "so long" or a "good-bye" to my mother. We only arrived at our destination Friday in the afternoon.

To reach my father's native village, it was necessary to cross a beautiful river by means of huge rocks lined up by nature in the middle of the water.

Some women were standing there bathing. They had long, beautiful hair that sparkled with the reflection of the sun; hanging carelessly down their body, it made them look feline. Some of them were rubbing their feet to remove callouses; others, seated, were massaging each other's backs. I threw an envious and sustained glance at their lovely, pointed breasts with dark nipples and brown aureolas; the sight of this nudity prompted me to touch and caress my own undeveloped breasts. I passed my hand first on one, then the other, as if I were imploring them to appear. I got a pleasant sensation from it.

Surprised at our arrival, the bathers automatically covered their pubes with their hands, crossing their legs and bending forward. Water was trickling over their satiny, copper skin; I would have liked to spend some time in the presence of these nude women, touch their breasts, see what effect my little hands would have. If I had dared, I would have asked them to let me run my fingers over the droplets. Just to see them run down . . . The women gave me a big smile. A toothless smile: their teeth were eaten away, broken, blackened. And, as if my disappointment could be read on my face, their smile shifted to a pout. I crossed the river without answering their greeting and, feeling lonely, rejoined my family.

I continued the journey with a sense of frustration, of disappointment. I followed a shaded path lined by a number of mango trees. Monkeys appeared: red, black, brown; they swung from branch to branch letting out their cries. The she-monkeys, with their babies hanging onto their bellies, moved me. I began thinking about Mama. I stopped to look at them. As if to entertain me and show me their suppleness, they gave a little demonstration of acrobatics with their babies hanging on. I was afraid I'd see them fall! A little further, the animals dug up tubers they ate accompanied by bird calls. The monkeys as well as the birds were chased by screeching little children with slingshots, or *laspeer*.* They put an end to the show. I had the impressions that the branches bent down to bid me welcome as I went by.

The path took me to a village surrounded by an enclosure of tree trunks into which a little gateway had been cut. The round huts with their thatched roofs were spaced at a distance from one another. The village, spacious but not very populous, had been hidden beneath the foliage of giant trees at the foot of a mountain that swallowed it up.

The gathering in front of the first hut made me understand that my roots were there. Like an automaton, I bent over to enter.

Seated by the fire, my grandmother was crying with joy and wanted to take us all onto her long legs. She was repeating *toli-toli*, welcome.

Grandfather was lying on a mat stretched out on a bed of hard earth; he was resting beneath a number of blankets even though it was very warm. He must have been quite sick. Since he wanted to be seen sitting up, he asked for help to sit up. I was struck by his light-colored skin, his curly hair, and his delicate features, which gave him a kind of Moorish handsomeness. I'm not sure what graceful quality in his glance predisposed a person to like him immediately. He had only to look at you, and you were instantly submissive, won over. I lowered my glance at once, but looked up again into his eyes.

This maneuver lasted only an instant. He held out such beautiful hands, with long, thin fingers, that I couldn't resist

*Slingshots [a Wolof word from French, "lance-pierres."—*Trans.*].

the temptation to massage them. His refined gestures betrayed innate distinction and elegance. He called me Bâata,* but couldn't tell my brothers apart.

Everyone was aware of our arrival; the generosity of the villagers was equaled only by their congeniality. Everyone came carrying a calabash with the special dish of the Fuuta-Jaloo, fonio,† or tubers and feculents of all sorts. The villagers wanted to shake our hands. Their hands were calloused from hard labor. Each person wanted news of some relative living in Senegal; the only city they knew about was Dakar, and they thought everybody knew each other, just as in their village.

I was quite tired by this long trip and the day full of new experiences and people. Women brought us water they had heated for our baths. I would have preferred to go to the river to bathe. I might have met some of those beautiful women who had quietly intoxicated me and who continued to preoccupy my thought.

I repeated sorrowfully, "Never will I see anything as beautiful as the nakedness of a woman."

After my bath, I wanted to sleep and, particularly, to remain alone, something that was difficult since the one wave of visitors was immediately followed by a wave of new people. After a long delay, Papa finally took me to a neighboring hut where two beds were in evidence, a big one and a small one.

"This place belongs to me, and I built it the year your mother and I were married."

I must have fallen asleep right away, without eating and with the thought that there was a story behind everything here. The following morning, I was awakened by the rooster's first crow. That first melody was really pleasant, with the accompaniment of the birds chirping and the cattle lowing! Nature's awakening was an entire symphony! Here everything was springing

---

*The favorite wife of a polygamous man. In Peul culture, a granddaughter is symbolically called the grandfather's wife and the grandson the grandmother's husband.
†A cereal grass with very fine grains.

to life—the grass, buds, first leaves. I went outdoors to see the birds, but without success. I took in great breaths of fresh air. I was particularly struck by the perfume of the citronella, an herb my father had just cut to prepare us an herbal tea for breakfast. I would have liked to run all around the surrounding area, but the dew held me back.

Everything was new for us. We were in a hurry to go out and touch everything. Alas! Visitors were on the lookout. We only knew how to answer yes or no. Most of the time, we were lost with the Peul language, with its melodious sonorities and rich vocabulary. We did not understand it very well except when Papa spoke to us, with his own words, as he had done in Dakar.

He was also a good storyteller, but we discovered some better than he was in this village. It seemed as if everyone took it upon themselves to have us relive history along with the habits and customs of the village. To belong to the village necessarily meant to know it and to transmit what one knew to the next generation. I would have liked for Papa to wait for evening to tell us stories, as he had in Dakar.

"You see that hut, it's made of clay. It is very cool inside; that's why we light a fire. That's too bad because the smoke yellows the wall, which is whitewashed. The ceiling, made of long bamboo, has a granary. After each harvest, a fire is lit to dry the corn, which keeps it from rotting. As for the floor, it has been made from a mixture of cow manure and sand. The women draw arabesques on it. The land is fertile, and the inhabitants are well-off with their land, which they rent in exchange for a portion of the harvest. They often cultivate part of it for themselves, just to keep busy. Your grandfather, the lazy fellow—may God forgive me!—was satisfied with renting all his land. He would spend his days sitting in the shade of the orange tree across from the hut, contemplating his hands, which had never been put to work. He indulged in generosity by passing out the harvests of your grandmother, the only one who worked relentlessly, without complaining, with the help of us children. That's why I went away at age ten to earn a living. I'll tell you about that part of my life one day, maybe. The Fuuta-Jaloo is a land of learned people while, for your grandfather, the only sura he seems to know without making serious mistakes are the "Fatiha" and the "Qoulhouallahou."*

"Your papa's very handsome—I like him."

"You've fallen under his charm. Everyone succumbs to it except us, his children. In any case, that is his only wealth. People judge only by appearances—too bad!"

I couldn't stay still any longer. I wanted to go out. It was ten o'clock by my watch. I mentioned that to Papa.

"You'd do better to take off your watch—you won't need it. Here, a simple glance is enough to let people know exactly what time it is."

"I'm keeping my watch; I'll never take it off."

"You can simply take it off your wrist and attach it, let's see, to one side of your pagne."

"I'll see."

I was really fond of this watch, a present from my father when I received a prize at the end of my second year of the elementary program. I never took it off day or night. This was my only treasure since Mama had taken away my *dibe.*

*Sura from the Qur'an.

My father finally let us go out. He led us to the village exit leading toward the mountains. Facing us, a field of fonio stretched as far as we could see. My brothers and I began running in all directions, raising more havoc than the monkeys people chased away. The peasants were very nice; they wanted to teach us how to hold a sickle and even explained the different stages for cultivating fonio, the food you digest so quickly you have the impression of never being full. You do not offer it to important guests; it's not even served for feasts, unlike corn and rice, which are not grown much in this region.

When we returned to the village, we weren't hungry any longer since we had eaten like primitive people, putting any kind of fruit in our mouths without knowing whether it was edible: the taste alone guided us.

As if they were compelled by duty, the villagers brought food for us. There were three groups: the women, the men, and the *bilakoro.** It was forbidden for the *bilakoro* to wash with the men in the river, which had separate zones (if the atmosphere was smelly, the *bilakoro* were accused of causing it). They couldn't play with the men either, but rather with my brothers, although they were often older.

When night fell, the moon was as bright as a torch—a lamp or an ember was hardly necessary to light your way. The young people would gather and, seated in a circle, tell stories or ask each other riddles.

Births were not registered—some important event would serve as reference. For example: the year of the great bush fire

*Uncircumcised men [a Malinke word designating not only lack of circumcision, but an outsider, a man who does not belong to the community—*Trans.*].

or the year of the good or bad harvest. This manner of calculating did not satisfy everyone—young men tried to prove their age by their superiority in wrestling. This was hand to hand, with no blows, and three rounds maximum. It was necessary to take the opponent down twice in a row and to immobilize him. The winner became the older one. If both antagonists fell or if one could not take his opponent down or immobilize him, they were the same age. The adversaries shook hands immediately.

Adolescents who had undergone their "rites of manhood" could no longer sleep in their mother's hut, but rather in the one they had built together. They went to the *hiirde** where there were *ñamakaala,*† who were invited or managed to get themselves invited. The boys could court the girls.

These wrestling matches of the *bilakoro* made me nostalgic for the *làmb* in Dakar—I preferred the latter by far for their beauty and nobility (no blows were given). Here, the important thing at stake was to enter the world of grown men.

Seeing these skinny runts come up against one another, you might think they would be broken into pieces. In reality, they were quite hearty, like reeds that bend but never break.

No resemblance to the living statues, those fighters of my childhood.

Before breaking up, the girls danced—happy and glowing. Their dances did not attract me, although I would have liked to be naked, or semi-naked like them. But I had been accustomed to the "civilization" of clothing. It was difficult for me to imitate these nubile girls, who tried to wiggle their budding breasts like women, the role they were destined to play.

These dances brought back the image of the women in the river, which had aroused my unsatisfied desire to feel breasts, real breasts, and to run my hand through long hair.

Later, when I saw exhibits of paintings and sculptures, my fingers always itched with a desire to run over the contours,

---

*An evening gathering.

†Troubadours, traditional singers.

to dwell on the forms. I still have a tactile, sensual relationship with art. In museums, I take a furtive glance around and then let me fingers slide, secretly, over the beauties as I think of those nymphs in my childhood. The sign "Do not touch" was surely invented for people like me . . .

The village was located in between three *luumo,** held on Tuesday, Thursday, and Sunday. The nearest market was two kilometers away; the most distant, fifteen.

On the first Tuesday after we arrived, my aunt was able to persuade me to go to market with her. She was an authoritarian woman with no children, and she directed all her love to us. She had taken for herself my little sister, who lived with her. Our arrival in Guinea was a gift from heaven for her: there she was, all of a sudden, the mother of five children. Being a very generous woman, she gave each of us a goat, a chicken, and several fruit trees—an orange tree, a banana tree, etc.—and we had to take care of them. If we had encouraged her, she would probably have given all her property to us.

She asked me to put on a scarf so I wouldn't have my head all red with dust. That must have been my first scarf. It made me look strange. My aunt thought I put it on just right.

So we left for the market. Here, people have the centuries-old instincts of nomads since they cover great distances on foot.

We ran into people dressed in clothes of glistening colors. Curiously, harmony of color was reserved for the men while the women dressed in clashing colors.

Everything was carried on the head, sometimes very heavy loads: baskets of cola nuts, cloth, doughnuts, *sumbara,*† fruits . . . Most of the people we met, especially the men, were wearing their shoes hanging from their shoulders by the knotted

*Weekly markets.

†A condiment made from a sweet fruit [particularly from the *nere* (Wolof), an African carob tree of the Mimosa family; note that the word is spelled *sumbala* in Malinke—*Trans.*].

shoelaces, and when they were plastic, they protruded from the baskets carried on the head.

This surprised me.

"Don't worry, it's nothing, they will put their shoes on."

"But when?"

"We're getting close to the market, I'll explain later."

A river was flowing close to the market. Beneath the bridge, people were taking off their dusty clothes, rinsing the dust off, and putting on their clean clothes. They were also putting on their shoes and, with their eyes riveted on them, were taking a few hesitant steps before entering the market with a satisfied look.

"Here, people 'dress' for the market—it's a time for meeting people. You will see."

"What an idea to have shoes and walk barefooted! Don't thorns and pebbles hurt them?"

"It's a matter of habit. Clothes are carefully kept. For sure, shoes are put on only for market days, a time to make an appearance, and then they are put away until another feast or market day. It's better to wear out feet rather than shoes."

This market was like a fair, very different from Dakar. Steers, sheep, goats, dogs, and many other animals were there. And each time the animals mated, curious onlookers gathered around to yell their own fantasies.

"Pick-ups" proceeded apace—beautiful women with babies on their backs were setting up rendezvous with this and that gentleman, or another a bit further away. Most of the time, their husbands were living abroad or had been absent for years!

"You're telling me they're married? You're not serious! I've just seen some ten women giving rendezvous to different men."

"They're not doing anything evil. It's just for the pleasure of being together, nothing else."

"It's strange, all the same, don't you think?"

"Here, love is different than what you find in the country

you've come from. All the girls are virgins until they get married, and yet they have boyfriends. "

"Aren't adolescent girls who let themselves be picked up and who are going to sleep outside of the hut scared? And don't their parents warn them?"

"That proves that nothing serious is happening. The lover is the moral guardian of his companion's virginity. Even married men flirt, despite the presence of their wives, you see, and they return home accompanied by their conquest. The wife receives the lover with full honors. The lover will sleep with the husband, and the wife has the choice of sleeping in a neighboring hut or in the same hut with the couple."

"Even in the same bed?"

"Of course not; she will sleep in another bed if there is one, or else on the ground. Or she will go to stay with friends. The next morning, she will prepare breakfast for the couple, and she will go to the river to get water for the lovers' bath. The lover may stay several days, and during her sojourn she will monopolize the husband. Relations develop between the women all the same. Stop judging and especially comparing—just observe. Be sparing of words and develop your sense of observation—you'll need it more than your mouth."

We returned to the village. I had taken back to my grandmother the cola nut somebody gave me in spite of my protests.

"It's not polite to refuse a gift, even if you don't want it. The cola nut is a symbol of friendship, of peace, of alliances, of marriage, of birth, of mourning. You'll see it at all the events of social life in the Fuuta-Jaloo."

In spite of her advanced age, my grandmother was happy to chew on her cola without grating it, using the few teeth she had left. My grandfather simply remained in bed. The state of his health did not seem to improve.

"How did you like the market?" asked my father.

"I didn't like it—it was too tiring: too many greetings, hands to shake; people calling me by my name, while I didn't know anyone. Most of the people spoke to me in Wolof."

I had never liked public places where everyone turns around to stare at you. I have rarely gone to the market. My aunt said that I had enjoyed a great success nonetheless, judging from the number of cola nuts she had received for me.

Days went by, and each of us tried to assist in some manner with the life of the family. My brothers and I did our best. Peasant habits are not acquired from one day to the next, but at the end of a long period of patience.

Little by little, we began wondering about the length of our "prolonged vacation." Papa tried to shelter us from the strangeness of our environment. We continued having breakfast as we had in Dakar: tea, coffee, hot chocolate, along with that novelty, citronella tea. Our provisions began to run out because most of the village ate with us.

"Respectable" gentlemen began to visit, asking for my hand. Apparently the candidates had personally noticed me on market day, or a member of their family who wanted me for a brother, a cousin, or an absent son. This was not the same game as in La Medina, where people, including my father's customers, called me "dear" or "miss," even as they predicted a radiant future. Nature seemed to delay my entry into a world to which they wanted me to belong. Some days, my breasts were as big as little lemons, but other times, nothing was there. Some girls in the village had already been married at twelve or thirteen years old.

Apparently unhappy, Papa still replied politely.

"Come on, she's just a kid."

Certain people were insistent, fearing that I might be given to someone else.

"We promise you to wait as long as necessary as long as the religious ceremony is celebrated. We will keep her 'in reserve' with her own family."

Others promised to keep me at home while waiting for me to mature, as would be done with any precious acquisition. I was shocked and outraged. I wondered what they wanted with me. What was this insistence?

I had never been present during the suitors' conversations with my father. This was an affair for men—women were excluded. Women didn't have to give their opinion and, even less, their consent.

My aunt did not leave the *leymadi** before the end of these conversations, which she came to report to me.

They were all convinced of their "social success." They

*Porch.

were transporters, big merchants. Most of them lived abroad, where they owned shops, taxis, or houses with "solid" walls. The villagers considered them rich. They were often married and looking for an educated wife as the crown to their success, since most of them were illiterate. With the proud intention to "acquire" that wife, they were willing to pay the necessary price to prove to their family and friends what they were capable of.

In addition, they rarely sent their children to school, and if they did, girls were excluded. Many of them felt they had succeeded in life without schooling (success was demonstrated by houses, a car, and, especially, the number of wives) . . . Others simply did not want their children, not even the boys, to know more than they did. A sort of leveling at the bottom. What was contradictory was that they liked to express themselves in the language of Victor Hugo, an author they would not have understood.

I was even privileged to have a messenger sent from Sierra Leone by a diamond dealer who wanted me as a third wife. Even at my age, I knew that I was not intrigued either by men with money or by those with power. The richest of men, if he were uneducated, would not interest me. I wanted nothing except to be allowed to exist in my own way.

My aunt arranged an interview with the wife of one of the suitors. One afternoon, I saw a young woman of affected elegance arrive wearing a bunch of gold jewelry. She spoke to me in familiar terms, thinking she was already in conquered territory.

In a pretentious manner, she began speaking French to me, detailing all the wealth of her husband and picturing for me a paradise on earth.

"I myself am an intellectual by profession," she continued. "I prefer by far to have you as a co-wife than someone else; in any case, I know that my husband will take other wives. You are young, beautiful, and I am sure that we will get along perfectly. That understanding is important to me, to us. I can assure you that you will go to the best private schools in Abidjan. Don't worry about your studies, you have my word. My husband confirmed this to me, moreover. When I left him this morning, he told me to be sure to discuss the necessary details of the marriage with your father."

I had not said a word. Everything in her pedantic speech, peppered with errors, irritated me, but I was polite enough to accompany her for a few steps before my aunt took over at the edge of the village. If I had been forced to speak with her, it would have been to ask her to leave immediately, before I lost my temper. I was to have frequent occasions to reenforce my mutism in this country in order to control myself. I am no diplomat. That's one of the busses I missed. I don't go for appearance; I simply am.

A bit later, I dove into the dictionary to look up "intellectual." To what profession did that correspond? I began reading and rereading the definition.

"She's an intellectual? What about me then, what am I?"

I had been able to measure her "intellectual" level by her speech: by indulgent standards, she would be in the first year of the elementary program, with a host of spankings to teach her to make fewer mistakes.

I had the privilege of receiving several more visits from the "intellectual." Each time, her husband's wealth increased tenfold. My attitude toward her did not change—it was a handshake when she arrived and a "*jaaraama*"* when she left again.

"How can I make a good diplomat out of you?" my aunt sighed. I'm going to have to initiate you through some rapid and intense means."

"A good hypocrite, sure!"

"Here, people don't necessarily need to speak to make themselves understood; a glance, a gesture suffices. It's not necessary to shock or to raise your voice. You have to manage to understand a glance, to read people, to see where they're headed, to sense them as an animal does."

*Good day, which also means "thank you."

She concluded with a forceful image.

"You have to learn to walk on people's wounds without hurting them."

"How's that?" I asked, mouth agape and wide-eyed.

"That's where diplomacy lies."

My aunt, who was inwardly dreaming of seeing me richly married, told me: "How can you say no to a noble who, in addition to all the rest, sends his own wife to plead his case? You must be expecting a king to follow."

I remained like a marble statue. She continued.

"You're right. I confess to you that I prefer the diamond merchant by far, but according to my intelligence, he's an old man, and a woman interests him only until she gives him two children. Afterward, he finds her too old and abandons her, with some fortune. Although he has repudiated them, his two wives insist on staying. The problem is that I am getting older, and I don't know whether I would be able to help you raise the children you would have with him."

My aunt, the seventh of eight children, was my grandparents' only living daughter. Infant deaths were frequent, and families often lost the first child between birth and two years of age. So my grandmother, after losing her first child, gave birth to four boys and then two daughters, who died one after the other. A passing traveler had predicted to my grandmother, pregnant with Yayé, that she would have a daughter and that the latter would live only if, from birth, a *baylo** was the godfather.

When the baby was born, they called for a *baylo,* who made the required sacrifices. He breathed into the ears of his goddaughter so that she would live by words that only he the initiate knew. He returned the seventh day, the day of the baptism, to give a name and take care of the baby.

Yayé grew up in a cocoon, protected by the spirits, God, the *baylo,* and her family. Her slightest desires were satisfied, since she must not be vexed. She would grow up with the idea that everything was due to her. It sufficed that she wanted something for her wish to be fulfilled.

Her greatest pain was that she had not had any children— the only thing that remained for her to wish, if you will.

I later learned that my aunt attributed "nobility" to the rich, while noble birth had always been the most important trait in the Fuuta-Jaloo. For her, you were noble if you were rich. She was allergic to the poor. She went as far as forgetting their names. Her own first cousin, who had left to make his fortune, came back empty-handed. Yayé buried her family relationship with him. She would only admit that their two grandmothers had been inseparable friends and that, by dint of referring to each other as "sister," they had ended up thinking they really

*Blacksmith.

were sisters. She did not hide that she had relations only with well-to-do people.

As one might expect, she had married a rich man who took two other wives. My aunt spent more time at her mother's than with her husband; so the two days a week she spent in her husband's village had become a chore. My grandmother had given up reminding her daughter of her conjugal duties. She managed to have her husband's herd of cattle transferred to her family. But her social life kept her from taking care of it.

Out of spite, she told me, "My greatest treasure is you, my nephews and my nieces. I wish that you might never live with a man without bearing him a child."

She gathered possession after possession. That was a sort of compensation. She always liked to acquire more, even if she had to sell it afterward. For us, she was divesting herself of her wealth.

She often repeated, "You know I'm not all that poor."

Riches were calculated by the number of head of cattle. She had never known exactly how many she had. Her husband must have known.

"You know, Papa told me that there was a certain Rockefeller, a very rich man."

"How many cattle did he have?"

"I don't know."

"So, when you tell me about how many head of cattle he has, I'll tell you if he is as rich as you say."

In every season, there was fire in my grandmother's hut. I liked to help relight it, uncovering some coals beneath the cinders, throwing some twigs on and blowing on them until I was out of breath.

"Blow hard on them."

My work did not satisfy her—she pushed me aside so she could set to work. Her bellows were no less hardy than those of the *baylo*.

This was the third Tuesday of our stay. Grandfather took advantage of his wife's absence that morning to arrange his great boubou, embroidered with gold thread, before arising, majestuous, and taking a few steps, supporting himself on the wall.

"You will not simply keep the image of an ailing, prostrate, bedridden grandfather," he told us proudly. "You are going to see me standing and walking. I have asked God so many times to wait until I see you before I take my departure. Now, I can give up my soul without regret."

He took his hand off the wall in order to find an equilibrium on his feet—then he walked to the door and returned to his bed. My brothers and I had gotten up to take these steps with him, and we were ready to help him if he faltered. We were afraid he might stumble into the fire or have a fatal fall. With a great smile of satisfaction, which he kept all day, he returned to lie down without any help from us. Everyone thought this was a sign of improvement in his health.

He passed away at twilight, with the setting of the sun.

It was the day of the *luumo*. As soon as the death was declared by the family, a man took a hunting rifle and fired a certain number of shots in the air. Another entered the relay with a *tabalde* (or *tabala*),* giving a beat that resounded over a great distance. This is how grandfather's death was announced.

*A large drum.

The tide of humans that flowed in proved that the message had been received, and in record time. Villagers came to present us with their condolences. The wake was presided over by my father's older brother, along with the other brothers and close friends.

This was the first time I had seen actors. The spectacle they presented could not be conceived by any stage director. This included housewives who pretended to faint, professional mourners who wailed without shedding a tear, acrobats who hopped and rolled on the ground, and the soothsayers who, according to what they said, had known that my grandfather was going to die from hearing an owl or some other bird of misfortune hooting . . . What a spectacle! This is how women fulfilled their duty of crying.

Those who were afflicted by the misfortune wept discreetly and with dignity.

Maintaining complete control of herself, my grandmother did not cry. Two years older than her husband, she had lived with him all her life, and now she was taking leave of him forever. She was sitting next to me, our legs touching. She let go of my hand in order to shake the hands of visitors, then grasped my hand again. I wasn't crying either. Mostly I felt sad for her.

Neighbors brought us food, which let us and our guests eat or snack, although the food we had prepared would have been enough. There was no respite for us until evening. Some people came at night and did not return home until after the burial. Others returned for the funeral rites.

The burial took place the next day; although they were very young, my brothers were going to attend. They did not cry. What they had learned during their rites of manhood had borne fruit: a man does not cry.

Three widows who were my grandmother's age stayed until the day after. They were going to help her put on her mourning attire. She had her beautiful, long, smooth hair, white as cotton, braided and rolled under a scarf. A veil was placed on her head. Then she received their instructions.

"You must not turn around to look at anyone; Monday and Friday will be the days for your bath in the river—we will accompany you along with a young virgin."

I was chosen. I ran out to go find my father in his hut, where he was staying with my brothers; I began crying with all the tears in my body.

"Now that your father is dead, when am I going to return to school as you promised me?"

"As soon as possible. You're going to have to wait, but it can't be too long. I'll take you to Labé, thirty kilometers from here; you will stay with some friends or go to Conakry. Give me some time."

When they didn't see me, the widows came looking for me as if I must obey an order with no argument and without asking for my opinion.

"You will sleep beside your grandmother from today on. We will leave tomorrow, and you will see us Sunday and Thursday evenings for four months and ten days. Tomorrow, we will go together for the first ritual bath of her widowhood."

I was going to sleep on that little bed of earth, hastily whitewashed, where my grandfather had died. The mats, covers, and clothes of the deceased had been washed by the women initiates. I didn't sleep. That bed was hard and narrow. The images of that day of mourning came back to me. The three women, lying on the ground, talked to my grandmother all night.

I was thinking about this new responsibility that I had just been given and that was going to last for the period of her mourning. And where were my studies in all that? I began to have serious doubts about my father's promise. The school year appeared to me to be lost. While waiting to understand better, I let my grandmother's strong hands massage my back. And yet I wanted to run away, to be somewhere else. I gently pushed her hands away in order to curl up by myself, to isolate myself like a sea urchin.

At dawn, as we were leaving for the bath, the widows warned me: "You will say nothing of what you are going to see."

Silence followed, and I did as I was told; when we returned from the river, we ate breakfast before the women left, only to return for the next bath.

For the first time, Grandmother began her day by filling a small calabash with water that she poured under the orange tree as she intoned some prayers.

"This is for the spirits," she said. "Our dead are not dead—they are among us somewhere; they see us, but we cannot see them."

This often came back to mind. She gave me some cola nuts to bury. The custom was that only a pure child who had never had sexual relations could carry out this ritual and only in that case would the nuts grow.

"They are going to grow," she said.

At each meal, she served a portion in the calabash, which she would give to the first person passing by. She also had a hollow stone into which she poured water so the birds could come to quench their thirst.

My father recalled some sura from the Qur'an for me to recite and took me once a week to kneel at the tomb of my grandfather; along the way, I would gather some nice flowers to decorate the tomb. This fresh tomb looked like a hill that, with the passage of time, would sink to the level of the ground, only to disappear as if it had never existed. As a child, I was struck by the sensation of human nothingness and futility as I looked at this spot where it all ended. Papa had told me that, but this time I saw for myself.

From that time onward, the life I was to lead would be full of mystery.

I have seen the world, but I always return to kneel there, at my grandfather's tomb. My sensation in the face of death remains the same. Those we love do not die; they simply exist somewhere, as I had been taught by Paty,* the person I love more than anyone.

---

*The name "Paty" evokes the Peul word for grandmother, *pati.*— *Trans.*

I have favorites. As for my grandmother, I loved her from the first day. I like her strong spirit, her tenacity, her hard work, her honesty, her wisdom, her selflessness, her mischievousness, her secret life. Her mastery over herself, over people and things. She is a great lady, adaptable, slender as a liana. She has the appearance of women aware of their own beauty. She threw her head backward when it was not inclined to one side or the other. This was no longer intended to display her beauty; the impact of time meant nothing to her. She saw her own reflection only in the river, having given up the use of mirrors years before.

I went everywhere with her. One day, before going out, I handed her a mirror, so small you had to place it in the palm of your hand to see yourself. This was one of the rare treasures found among my grandfather's effects.

Refusing to look at herself, she told me: "By looking at you, I know how I should be. It's impossible for me to be and to have been."

"But how can you live without ever looking at yourself in a mirror?"

"To see what? One's faded beauty? What for?"

"For the pleasure of seeing yourself, what can I say?"

"Seeing myself? But I see myself in you. I have to be ugly so you can be so beautiful. And you must be telling yourself, this old woman, faded and wrinkled, must never have been young or beautiful, right? Too bad your grandfather isn't here any more—he would tell you what a beautiful girl I was. I was you and, with luck, you will be me. You see, growing old isn't a burden, but a privilege. Many people die too soon, often in the bloom of youth; when you have a chance to grow old and to be in good health, you must be happy."

I didn't persist, and for all the time I remained with her, I ended up not looking at myself anymore and seeing my own reflection only in the river. This was enough for me.

Grandmother was healthy and hard-working—she had energy to sell. She made her own soap and spun her cotton thread, although her children kept her in clothes. She grew vegetables. She made her own butter from cow or sheep milk. Part of it was melted and used for cooking; the other part was used for her hair, to give it a beautiful luster. Through barter, she exchanged calabashes full of milk for others filled with cotton, corn, and other goods.

I helped her with her daily work—and neither the weather nor the season changed that. But she never asked anybody for anything. Work could be delayed, but never forgotten, not even if each season brought something additional to be done. Grinding, for example, was a daily task. Only the type of grain was different. When one task was done, we went on to the next one. We went from one place to another, just as the sun goes on its celestial route. My grandmother didn't have to tell me to work—I couldn't imagine watching her work without helping her. I have never been able to see someone working without participating. I wanted to make the most of the time I could be with her, as if we were going to be separated forever, from one instant to the next.

Although she was talkative, she could spend entire days working without unclenching her teeth. She shared her meals only with the people she really liked. When a visitor was not to her liking, she was deaf. I began speaking louder, which I hate doing, so she would hear me.

"You know," she said, "you don't have to yell—I hear perfectly well, but since I began making people think I am deaf, I have been quite content. Silence does not bother me; before you came, I practiced *gumree** all the while I was working."

I laughed—I had just understood where my bad character, my mutism had come from. We shared so many silences. We

*Not speaking from sunrise to sunset.

must belong to the species that fears wounding people with words. Here, feelings are not to be shown, but to be inferred.

She was my only friend.

The dry season was the most difficult time to bear; it was the period for oranges, which made our breakfast. Someone would climb the tree to shake the branches, and we would go to work collecting the fruit in our pagnes and baskets. Seated in my grandmother's spotless courtyard, under the orange tree, each one of us, equipped with a knife, a sickle, a hatchet, or a machete, managed to cope with this château of fruit. Thanks to our expert hands, and with extraordinary swiftness, we removed serpentine peelings. After taking in so much vitamin-rich fruit, we could face the day's hard work.

We covered great distances in order to find springs; the wells my uncles had dug were drying up. We had a hard time believing that the wide, beautiful river, which roared during the rainy season to display its strength, could dry up. (On the other hand, there were years when floods swept away the villagers' harvests, their huts, and their herds.) We had to store water for ourselves as well as for the cattle. The grass was scorched and crackling when you walked on it. At the same time, Grandmother looked for tender leaves for the cattle, who could no longer find grass. The cows had no more milk, and nurslings were dying. Powdered milk, which was sold at the market, had become part of our routine, and nursing women had to accept it.

Since water was rare and hygienic customs could not be followed, diarrhea increased the infant mortality rate.

Our day began with the rooster's first crow, accompanied by the dew of that frosty, penetrating coolness from the mountains. As her only warm garment, Grandmother threw on a second pagne woven from blue, black, and white cotton—this was called a *leppi*.

First, we went to look for cow manure that she used as fertilizer for her garden. Several baskets and several trips were necessary. Then we went to the river where, with *ñeduɗe,** we took water to fill her jug and my bucket. I took advantage of the occasion to wash in the fresh water of the spring, which woke me up completely. Grandmother walked straight with her jug balanced on her head and her arms hanging. I came afterward, admiring her agility and the noble angle of her head, which I was unable to imitate for fear my bucket would fall. Then, without losing any time, we left for the stable; I handed her the calabashes while she went to get the calves that were separated from their mothers at night. Then as she began milking, she talked to the cows and caressed them.

"Don't show them you are afraid—they would notice it. Caress them, be tactile—you can only tame animals with caresses, don't ever forget that. That's how I do it, even with you."

I burst out laughing.

"They accepted being milked with you here," she continued, "when they might have refused. Someone who loves milk as much as you do should know how to milk."

This initiation was not a success. I admit that I was really scared of horned animals. But I liked the calves. I would have preferred that they never grow up. I kept my distance until my grandmother finished milking and gave me a calabash of warm

*Small pots.

milk. With a straw, I got rid of several hairs that had fallen in. Then I wet my lips with the precious liquid and gulped it down by the mouthful. This was my first meal of the day. The lunch of the day before paled by comparison.

"Don't empty the calabash—there are mothers who are expecting some for their babies."

In common belief, the more you give, the more you receive. She gave this milk generously to these mothers, who fed it to their babies right away. Any who resisted were held vertically, with their noses pinched by two fingers, and force-fed as soon as they opened their mouths to breathe.

When Grandmother mentioned her cattle, her cows in particular, it was as if she were speaking of people; she had given them beautiful names. At sunset, to get them to come in, it was necessary to go after them, caressing and cajoling them. They would hardly ever return of their own accord. Like true females, and with a certain coquetry, they always had to be pleaded with, even when they wanted to move. For their part, the bulls returned by themselves, unless they had been seduced.

"You know, I tell them about every important event—a birth in the family, a death. They even know who you are—I spoke to them about you and told them that you were far away in an unknown country and that, no doubt, you would come to see us some day."

Dialogue existed between animals and humans, a very strong and touching relationship. No individual wanted to give up this link—only if the human judged that the animal's survival was unlikely or in case of necessity. Such as when it was necessary to make a sacrifice in the case of someone's death.

Not all parts of the animal were eaten by everybody: a certain part was for women, another for men. The *bilakoro* received only the intestines. Besides, people preferred to buy their meat at the *luumo* rather than to eat that of their own cattle. Out of respect for their animals, some people did not eat meat or consumed very little. They were vegetarians without realizing it, as a result of their love. But superstition was not lacking in their behavior. If one expressed a desire to eat meat, that inevitably brought about the death of an animal . . .

Grandmother took on varied tasks: if she was a veterinarian for her cattle, she was also the barber and the coiffeuse for all the village men, whom she sheared, so to speak. She claimed that her trembling hands no longer allowed her to be the official midwife.

She ate little and never at the home of others, and she did not take part in meals at feasts.

She always said, "You must eat at home before going on a visit."

Eating a meal with her was something of an exploit. Those she invited preferred to decline since her advice on anything and her reflections killed the appetite. You had to eat with your fingertips, in very small quantities and take time to chew with the mouth closed before putting your fingers back in the bowl; it was obligatory to wipe your mouth before drinking from your bowl. This ceremony took place in the silence of the dead. Anyone who had the misfortune to let the act of chewing be heard would remember it. "You would think a herd of bulls was crossing through a mud swamp!"

She was content simply to put in an appearance at ceremonies she was obliged to attend. At baptisms, she went home the moment the name was announced, without drinking or eating.

All our errands were done on foot. I was her cane, she liked to say. I would have preferred she got into one of the rare passing trucks, which were overloaded and went zigzagging along. The drivers of these vehicles would accelerate in order to pass in the most dangerous circumstances, which gave them the reputation of being a good driver and brought them a large clientele. As a motto at the front of the cabin, there was an insignia in large letters: "DEATH DOESN'T GIVE A DAMN."

I had convinced grandmother to get into one of these trucks

with me. I went to bargain with the driver, who accepted letting the two of us sit beside him.

Grandmother waited for me in the shade of a tree, and at some distance from the truck, which she didn't want to approach for anything in the world. At least, not alone.

"The driver will take us, and we can sit beside him in the cabin. We're going quite a distance."

"It's far when you go by car, but I know some shortcuts, some paths the truck cannot take."

"You won't notice the distance by truck, I assure you, and you won't be tired when we arrive."

"You know, I confess that I've never gotten into one of these heaps of iron. I don't trust them. I have a friend, a woman who traveled in one to go see her daughter in Labé. It was horrible! As the truck went along, she had the impression that the trees moved aside, which made her dizzy and caused her to vomit. For the return trip, she put a veil over her head so she wouldn't see the trees moving. She swore she would never repeat the experience."

"You always told me that the *porto*,* the inventor of the needle, did good things. This heap of iron, as you call it, was born from his genius."

"Yes, that's true. The needle is useful. But it has never killed anybody. It allows me to sew my pagnes to size, as soon as the weaver sends me a rolled-up piece of cotton fabric. Only its other use is arguable. You know, when the *porto* wanted to stick large needles into our bodies to avoid an epidemic, like a lot of other people, I didn't go: for me, real illness is sticking a needle into your skin. What an idea! As long as I live, there won't be any needles in me, and I will trust my feet more than the moving heap of iron. Have you thought about accidents?"

"Let's get on the road now, before the sun gets hotter and the serpents come out of their holes to get a tan."

And there we were, my grandmother going ahead with me behind her, trying to follow her great strides. She was discon-

*A white person.

certing. But I understood that, for her, this invention was one of the greatest catastrophes.

Later, when I returned from my stays in France, I always went to spend my vacation with her.

When I was leaving, she would tell me: "When you come back, be careful crossing the street. It seems that the automobile was invented in the country where you're living."

She repeated her advice on cassette, the only way I had to remain in contact with her. My father would record her in secret, afraid that she would react to this other new invention as she had to vaccination and the automobile. The recorder, for her, was the parrot of the *porto*.

"I promise to be careful."

When there was a big fire in the bush, the only airplane that flew over the village was a tanker plane that came to extinguish the fire. Grandmother stopped her work in the field and told everybody that her granddaughter was in it, because they had told her that I took the airplane to go to Europe.

Everyone who entered her house had to take off their footwear. She had several calabashes. Each one had its own use: to store cereals, to hold milk curds, to use as a bank or a suitcase. Another calabash, covered with a large winnowing basket she had made, served as her "suitcase." That is where she stored her clothes, after having folded them.

Astonished, I asked her, "Why don't you put your clothes in one of the suitcases you have?"

"Those things are too complicated. One day, your aunt put my clothes in one. I couldn't open it when I was supposed to attend a baptism."

"Maybe the suitcase was locked—didn't you have the key?"

"According to your aunt, it wasn't locked—I just had to press on something."

"Your clothes are going to be rumpled where they are, and I could help you open the suitcase if you have problems the next time."

"You don't realize, perhaps, nor your aunt either, but the clothes I put in the calabash serve to fool people around me. The clothes I really need are on the bed. I place goat or sheep skins on it, and once my clothes are neatly folded, I finally put one or two blankets on top. My clothes are spotless and the bed is not so hard for you . . . But at night, you wiggle around like a real little devil, and you rumple everything . . ."

"I promise to try to thrash around less at night so I don't wrinkle your clothes . . ."

When someone occasionally bought a calabash of milk from her, she put the bills in the bottom of a calabash holding fonio, corn, or something else, and then she found her money gnawed by insects or reduced to powder.

The villagers received this money from relatives abroad. But they didn't need it very much. They only used it to buy salt.

Grandmother could have done nothing. Everyone helped her, including her married children and fathers with a family along with their wives, who went to get water and wood for her and even ground food for her. Her daughters-in-law made it a duty to bring her the food she needed. The old woman was content merely to line up the calabash and the bowls of food that she didn't eat, since she always did her own cooking. And she returned their dishes by serving them to the offspring of the daughters-in-law or, if they didn't visit, to any person who happened to pass by.

Grandmother developed a theory to which all the villagers adhered: "When the stomach is full, it summons the spirit, which loses its awareness of the most important things in life." She had ideas that were her very own and that allowed no discussion. In her opinion, only the slothful ate too much and could stay in bed mornings. As long as one lives, one should sleep only a reasonable amount. We have all eternity to sleep as long as we want without fear of being disturbed.

On several occasions, I reproached her for her manner of sleeping.

"You sleep all doubled up and that doesn't leave room for me."

"You only sleep with your legs stretched out when you have a full stomach. Doubled up, you don't bother anyone, even if your stomach growls."

"What's keeping you from eating what you want? There's enough to eat, isn't there?"

"I've told you that the body has to be trained—the stomach is like the rest. Everything depends on what you're accustomed to."

"In any case, I don't have room. I'm not going to sleep with you any more. I'm going to sleep in the hammock or go back to father's hut, where I'll have everything and, especially, a decent bed for me alone."

But my grandmother had her own ways, ingratiating and infallible, for giving orders and getting her own way. You gave in to her without even realizing it—her appearance of being an unassuming woman was deceptive.

She managed to get me to give up the idea of the hammock. She didn't like to see me in it since that is where I lay when I was in the grips of doubt or anxiety. That was my refuge—I would swing more and more quickly, until I was exhausted, and I felt better afterward. I used that hammock so much that I really wore it out.

Grandmother gave me three fingers of honey every morning. To calm me, she would say. A strange feeling would take hold of me. I would keep her finger in my mouth a long while and I ended up sucking her middle finger, after repressing the impulse to bite it.

"I know you want to bite me. Can you tell me why?"

"I don't know."

"In that case, just let it remain an impulse, nothing more."

She wanted to keep me with her, and she succeeded. Everything gave in to her. I loved for people to take care of me, and she knew it. Every evening, without the knowledge of my aunt (who found me capricious and too soft—I suspected her of being jealous of my grandmother's treatment), my grandmother gave me prolonged massage sessions. She passed her hands over the flames in order to make the shea butter she spread on them melt, and then she rubbed them all over my body, from head to toes, making my joints crack. She massaged my hands too—from the palm to the ends of my fingers—and then my scalp from the back of my neck to my forehead, and from my forehead to the back of my neck with circular movements of her firm farmer's hands.

"Your skin is dry—it drinks up all the shea butter," she complained. "I hope I can manage to make it soft as a baby's."

I wanted to tell her to go ahead since I was hers—I let myself go.

In the evening, I always pretended to be too tired in order to tempt her to go to work on my body, which she polished and worked over, stopping only when she was satisfied that it was smooth.

Grandmother would feel my forehead several times during the day; as soon as she found it hot, she would sense the beginning of an illness, which had to be stopped before it went too far. She would take out her great pot of baked clay, fill it with herbs, bits of wood, and other ingredients. You only had to tell her the symptoms of the illness for her to find a remedy. I would escape her medications by pretending I had aches and pains, since I preferred the masseuse to the healer.

Papa said, "There is a danger that Néné, with all her mixtures, may blow up the hut. She makes a veritable bomb."

In the middle of one night, the pot, filled with various and diverse soaking ingredients, did explode. The infernal noise woke us up. We quickly relit the fire and picked up the herbs, leaves, and bits of wood scattered around. Grandmother contemplated the pieces of her pot.

Sorrowfully, she said, "I can't throw them away—that would be too ungrateful. That pot served me for years. Your grandfather, all my children, not to mention the neighbors, were all cared for thanks to the pot's good and loyal services."

One man in the village intrigued me—he appeared to be age-less, although people had told me he was my father's age. He was not attractive in his physique, with a mouth set back and opening onto a jutting chin. You could see only one tooth, an incisor; it was large and resembled a hoe. Any other person in his place would have avoided smiling, but he ostentatiously displayed his tooth. He went to the market only to buy bread; he would cut a piece off, since he couldn't chew it, and begin sucking it right away. For hours, this piece of bread was shuffled from one side to the other and pressed against his palate. His nostrils quivered, and he would caress his goatee as a mark of satisfaction.

He had the piercing look of people from around here.

He was a child of the village, but he lived outside, on a hill. He was called Karamoko (without anyone being able to say whether he had studied to deserve this title of "master").*

My grandmother and I were among the few people to whom he spoke. With the men of the village, he only exchanged a laconic *jaaraama*. Not accepted in the area, not invited to any ceremony, nobody had anything to do with him.

Some people detested him; others ignored him; everybody agreed that he was crazy.

From the moment we arrived in the village, as other suitors were pushing each other aside, he foretold my future, holding my hands.

"Don't be afraid, you won't marry any of them. You will go back to your native country, with the *porto*. You will be famous. Your first child will be a boy."

*The name "Karamoko" is the word for "master" or "marabout"— *Trans.*

Before he had finished, my grandmother pulled my hands out of his, ordering him not to speak to me any more and to leave.

What people reproached Karamoko for was due to his father. It was a long time ago. The village had some large land holdings, and some wise men had gathered to ensure an equitable distribution of land: the villagers were to go out of their dwelling at the first crow of the rooster, and the limit of their land would be established at the point where they met each other.

Karamoko's father had begun walking after the last evening prayer. At the first crow of the rooster, he was already at the concession of other people, before their very door. He demanded that the property line be established there and nowhere else.

After that, people had managed, by occult means, to make him fart so strongly and so often that he could not go anywhere. He died of shame. His son Karamoko inherited the paternal failing. The village refused to give him a girl to marry and refused even to seek one in another village. He thought the most beautiful girls were in his village.

Rumors also circulated about his powers as a healer. These rumors occasioned his exclusion from the mosque. On the other hand, all the surrounding villages called him and even attributed unlimited powers to him: to put a hex on someone, to call down lightning, to bring paralysis or death to someone, or to cause the person to lose a limb . . . As for his good deeds, they consisted principally of healing women's sterility . . .

Bora was one of his patients. She was a woman from the neighboring village. She had been married less than a year. Her marriage was the first I attended. She was beautiful and wore large pearls crossed between her breasts, jewels of gold, and large bills pinned on her forehead. The guests danced, sang, and lived it up. Gossips had doubts about her virginity, given her brazen character. The wiser people said that, on the wedding night, her husband had no scratches but that the next morning he had a bandage on his big toe: to save his wife's honor, he may have voluntarily wounded himself in order to leave several drops of ritual blood on the little white pagne that is displayed as a proof of virginity.

The week after the marriage, the family accompanied Bora to the conjugal house, gave her some seed for her garden (an exclusively feminine domain) and for her field as well as some kitchen utensils and a *waramba leppi** for the husband.

But no child came, which was a cause of humiliation for her and even of possible repudiation: sterility is a sanction from God, a failing, a mark of uselessness.

So rumors were flying; her parents and those of her husband were beginning to worry.

In fact, marriage is a matter for parents; it is an alliance between two families whose will the bride and groom simply have to carry out.

Bora was not much older than I was, and already she was being reproached for what nature was refusing to give her. Her mother wanted to know whether things were all right, without daring to utter a forbidden word.

"Are relations between your husband and you normal?"

"Yes, everything is fine."

"I have confidence in you, but I have doubts about my son-in-law's fertility. The day after your wedding night, the covered calabash containing your little blood-spattered pagne came back to your grandmother. I confess that we expected a 'tarot' leaf'† instead. This man, who had remained a bachelor for too long, has never been known to consort with a woman, and there has long been the rumor that he is unable to satisfy a woman. It has always seemed suspicious that his family had not married him off. When he finally decided to take a wife, your father accepted his request. I made a number of sacrifices to prevent the marriage from taking place. In vain. But after all, if he has had relations with you, he ought to have children.

*A great man's boubou in woven cotton.
†The leaf of a tuber [*ñàmbi*, manioc—*Trans.*] which, once picked, grows soft: this symbolizes impotence.

In that case, we must go see Karamoko to exorcize the bad luck."

The husband underwent the same questioning from his father. He returned home without speaking to his wife. He did not eat and went to bed on the ground; this was an alarm signal, meaning that something was bothering him and that he was not content. This behavior went along with his refusal to fulfill his conjugal duty.

Her husband's attitude did not displease Bora, since it was a chore to make love to this person who, moreover, had been imposed on her by her father.

This rustic fellow was an inveterate worker; early in the morning, as the dew appeared, he left his home to work his field and did not return until evening. His wife took his midday meal to him, and he shared it with other peasants. He returned at sunset, exhausted, but carrying bundles of firewood or big logs that he gave to his wife. He did not take time to clean up or to remove his dirty clothes and put on clean ones. He collapsed like an old sack of potatoes and fell asleep snoring.

His wife refrained from waking him to eat for fear that the animal might experience other needs.

Bora often remained awake all night, since it was impossible to sleep beneath the same roof as this snorer, who could be heard at a great distance. People told her that it was only a matter of habit, that she would get used to it. She did not get used to it.

The husband's hunger strike continued. When the council of wise men was called together to discover for what the husband was reproaching his wife, he said nothing. The sages did not persist and awaited another occasion to clarify the situation.

After several days, the husband finally decided to speak to his wife, after having awakened her in an abrupt manner in the middle of the night.

"Go see Karamoko about the child: my parents are hounding me and asking me to marry another woman. I hope that you will give me a son who will succeed me and carry on my name! Having girls is fine, but they cause too many problems and do not leave any inheritance behind. It is as if they had never existed!

When all the children were girls, the father would give them boys' first names, to help heaven, and expecting the next would be a male . . .

Bora's husband was thinking about all of that. Overcome by sleep, he climbed into bed and fell asleep beside his wife, who remained awake, thinking about what she had heard from her in-laws.

"You serve only as an ornament in the house; you are not a woman, but a piece of furniture."

One had to avoid being seen when one went to visit Karamoko. That could alter or counteract the remedy he gave you. So, at dawn, the ideal moment for taming the spirits, as people said, Bora went to his place.

She was veiled for fear of being recognized by the early birds. She knocked three times.

"Bisimilla,"* replied Karamoko.

She went in. They engaged in the usual greetings.

"I know what brings you, my good woman. I have shown what I could do with most of those who have come to see me. I won't mention any names, as you know. But I must tell you that this is work that requires several sessions. My specifications must be followed to the letter. Otherwise, no positive results!"

He went to put on a special costume: a mask with cow horns and some cowries† sewn on the coat splotched with cola nut stains. He interrogated the spirits, whom he alone could see, then engaged in dialogue with them. Only the whites of his eyes could be seen. He continued with his incantations. In what language? Nobody knew. He threw the cowries in a winnowing basket and described his enemies without ever pronouncing their names. Each time that he hesitated to reveal a diagnosis, he scratched his bare cranium. Finally, he scribbled something

---

*The Peul spelling of an Arabic word meaning "welcome."
†The cowry shells were formerly used as money.

on an *alluwal* and poured some water over it, catching the liquid in a calabash.

"You will sleep on this *alluwal*," he stated.

The *alluwal* was so small that Bora could only sit on it. Suddenly, Karamoko, who was not wearing underwear, lowered his baggy trouser, dipped his penis in the vessel, and walked toward her.

"Don't say anything! This will seem bizarre to you, but it is the remedy. This is the only way to make you fertile. And especially don't think that I am taking advantage of you. Your husband should take the same preparatory measures each time he is going to have sex with you."

She hesitated a few moments, then went ahead. This man, who inspired fear, could certainly only do good.

She was wearing two pagnes, one large one and a small one that served as panties. Karamoko undid them, without completely taking them off.

When he had finished, he repeated, emotionless, his recommendations as if nothing had happened between them, without looking at her, as Bora tried to regain her equilibrium. He raised his baggy trouser and closed it with a precise gesture. He sat back down on a goat skin in a yoga position.

"Let your husband," he emphasized, "not fail to dip his organs in this water, before anything else. As for payment, people make no payment until they see the result. Meanwhile, your husband will bring me a goat and a mat before the next session, which is to say next week."

As he walked her to the door, and as if he just remembered something, he said, "Oh! And don't forget that the result of what we have just begun could be compromised if there were any indiscretion. The spirits like discretion."

Following the session, she walked homeward, still veiled. Her husband was waiting to find out how the consultation had gone and if there were sacrifices to be made. Quite tired, Bora gave him the bottle filled with the fertilization liquid that Karamoko had given her.

"You must wet yourself with this before doing anything," she said simply.

Her husband replied with a broad smile, expressing a certain satisfaction, which irritated his wife.

"He has the reputation of being a good healer—he knows the entire village and its problems. I have complete confidence in him. We must follow his recommendations to the letter."

Bora stretched out, waiting for the dew to dissipate so she could go work in her vegetable garden. All day long, she thought about what she had undergone. It did not seem normal to her. She would have liked to speak with her husband about it, but fear kept her from doing that, all the more since her husband venerated Karamoko. She did not ask whether her husband knew about his much-vaunted practices . . .

How could she speak about this without indiscretion? And to whom? Karamoko had recommended discretion. So she told her mother. The latter reassured her.

"We're going to talk about this between us women," she said. "All the women who have gone to see Karamoko have tread the same path, right? So what are you complaining about? Go to the consultations, which will become more and more frequent. At each session, he will vary his methods according to what I have been told. When he is tired of you, he will ask you to caress him: the sperm gathered will be an ingredient for the fertilizing mixture."

"Mama, do you think these are normal practices?"

"I don't know. How can we know? All I know is that I want you to remain married, not to be repudiated. If this is the price to pay, tell yourself that you are not the first."

"I detest Karamoko. He is dirty and repulsive—he only washes on Friday for the principal prayer. The only clean spot he has must be his buttocks given the ablutions he must carry out before turning toward the Lord to invoke his mercy!"

"Forget this monster! Get ready to face him and think about your objective—to have a child. Go along with it as if you liked what he's doing."

Bora returned often to see Karamoko, as foreseen. She accepted everything her mother had predicted. Finally, she became pregnant. This much-wanted pregnancy reinforced the prestige of the thaumaturge, Karamoko. To top it all off, the child born of this illicit commerce was a boy. The husband spoke about it with pride. His paternity blinded him: he had eyes only for the baby, in whom he found some resemblance. As for Bora, she was delighted and fulfilled to have a baby, but she remained silent about the miracle recipe of the master who had cared for her. To speak about it would have been treachery and disloyalty. Karamoko had warned her that the spirits like discretion . . . To betray them might bring sanctions and perhaps the loss of this child whom she cherished. At the least bruise, Bora came to my grandmother to have her care for him.

As soon as she left, grandmother would tell me, "This is another of Karamoko's miracles. What can we do?"

That is how I became friends with Bora.

The men who had beautiful wives, isolated by their pride, were secretly envious of the healer because he saw so many young beauties come under his care, with husbands remaining in the wake.

The polygamous husbands were the most critical of Karamoko. In fact, their wives, who under normal circumstances should replace each other in the husband's company, sometimes formed a coalition so that none of them would fall into his arms in the kaïborou.*

Without being able to complain to anybody, of course, the husbands found on those somewhat bitter days that Karamoko had the best role: pleasures without obligations. Those days, they really resented Mody Caro, alias Karamoko.

*The husband's permanent residence, where his wives take their turns staying with him. The husband does not go to his wife except during the honeymoon.

The days went by, slowly. The free time that I took for myself was spent reading the few books I had brought from Dakar. I knew them by heart from reading and rereading them. Fortunately, I have always liked to read. I read everything that I found. I lived the lives of the characters. They were my great companions. They could make me laugh or cry. With them, I could escape. Thanks to them, I was never bored. They allowed me to fulfill my desire to know, which is still not completely satisfied.

To assuage his conscience, Papa bought me the *Horoya** to keep me busy, but it arrived several weeks after publication. The ink was so poor it blackened my hands, and the characters had disappeared at spots. The words and discourse that flowed most often from the pen of the journalist were "counter-revolution"; "down with imperialism, colonialism, and neocolonialism"; "long live the father of the nation, Sékou Touré"; "borders are closed until further orders"; etc.

I understood none of that and turned to my dictionary to look for the meaning of these words. No use. I finally gave up the search and continued to read simply to pass time, but nothing in that newspaper encouraged me to take it as my breviary. As for the old yellowed dictionary, almost reduced to tatters, I went through it, memorizing entire pages to enrich my vocabulary, which was so useless in this village.

*The Party newspaper, which spoke only of the government's policies.

My father encouraged me to write to my friends in Dakar. He took charge of getting my letters to them. I could use new words to impress them.

When they didn't answer, Papa told me, "Pretend they replied and answer them as if they had."

I did that. In this isolated place, there was no pen—I used soot from the pots, and with the pupils of a coranic school, we made it into ink. As for my pen, it was simply a reed sharpened with a razor blade. I began writing with exceptional concentration. I read my letters aloud to my father. He appreciated the content even as he deplored the writing.

My grandmother ended her mourning. Sacrifices were made, and a steer was killed. It was feast time, and people stuffed themselves with all sorts of food.

This was the moment when Papa left for a meeting with the minister of commerce, whom he had met in Dakar, where the latter was studying. He returned three weeks afterward, with overflowing enthusiasm. I even got a marvelous declaration of love from him. The first in my life.

"You know, I love you so much that I would like to gulp you down, keep you inside, and take you out each time to have you beside me. But I have to leave for Dakar without you. I am sending you to Conakry to stay with my friend the minister. We agreed on this. I prefer by far to confide you to his care rather than to leave you with my business friends in Labé.

The important thing was to get back to school. Whether that was thanks to the indulgence of a minister or not, in Dakar or somewhere else, did not matter to me. In my enthusiasm and joy, I even forgot the time I had lost—and to ask him what a minister was. Papa's revelation had put a healing balm on my heart. I went as far as forgiving him for having tricked me into coming to Guinea. I also wanted to tell him that I loved him, but something held me back, a sort of paralyzing timidity that has remained with me. I'll never know how to say those things. But it's great to hear them from the mouth of someone you love.

My father's love, the care he had taken of us, of me, the enthusiasm that he had shown each time I spoke to him of what I planned to do later—all of that refreshed my heart. Everything that I did, every idea that I mentioned to him, got his attention. The dialogue that took place between us was that of adults, when I was still a kid. He believed in me, which contributed to my blossoming.

My dream, alas, evaporated the day following that declaration of love, because I had been deceived again. Blinded by love, I had simply forgotten that I was dealing with a "merchant of illusions."

In fact, Papa was going to abandon me there, without enrolling me in any school or sending me to Conakry as he had promised. He left for Dakar by foot, since the borders were still closed and the border police had received orders to fire on anything that moved. I refused to tell him goodbye, since I did not understand the motives that had led him to leave me there nor the sense of danger that a clandestine border crossing represented.

Another disappointment—I was stupefied to discover that the correspondence I intended for my friends in Dakar had been buried at the bottom of my father's suitcase, beside the journal my mother had kept when she was pregnant with me. I hate being misled—I'll never like that. I climbed to the top of the great tree that overlooks the village and stared at the road leading toward Dakar. With my eyes, I swept the horizon as any landowner would have done with his property. I was not crying. I could not understand my father. All his utterances— "as soon as possible" and "any time"—were stricken from my vocabulary. Still today, it sows doubt in my mind to hear them. I understand that those formulas mean nothing.

I did not come down from my tree until nightfall and, for the first time, I went to sleep at the place of a woman in the neighborhood. I hardly knew her, but she recognized me; she was Bora's mother, the first person I encountered in my helplessness. Her welcome was warm. She did not ask any questions.

I loved this father—he was the "father-hen," and he was so present in my life and in the lives of my brothers that it had not occurred to us to miss Mama. And yet, I wanted to forget him as I had forgotten Mama. As soon as nice memories came back to mind, I shook my head violently to make them disappear. It is painful to be abandoned for reasons you don't understand. I will always have the sense of having been abandoned. And I have always suffered a lot from that. "I love you, but I am abandoning you." I couldn't understand. From that day on, I really felt that I was an orphan. Learning to live without the person you love . . . What use is there to live without being loved?

I couldn't swallow any more. My throat was all knotted up—food gave me the feeling of being strangled. I felt a burning sensation in my stomach. Grandmother forced me to eat some porridge—liquids were easier to swallow to get me through this "way of the cross." The pain was in my plexus. I was victim to insomnia and palpitations, just as when Mama had taken me back to my father's. I had my grandmother touch my heart.

"Look, it's beating so hard I have the impression it will come out of my chest."

For a long time, I had the idea that Papa would come back to get me and to explain his behavior. How many times I followed a stranger, thinking I had recognized Papa . . . I would live waiting for that cherished person, not wanting to latch onto anything, to anyone, except to the one who had left. I was going to follow this model in my adult life, to flee each time that I felt good, for fear of being abandoned once more. I remain a woman-child. I have not been able to grow up. I look for the person who was the man of my life in all the men I meet. I have not found him. Men think they are dealing with a woman, but in my mind, I am the child for whom time is frozen . . . looking for my father.

I was looking for you, having dialogues with you, and the same question kept coming back. Why did you abandon me? I wanted to disappear, never to give another sign of life. But I had a moral commitment to my sister and brothers; I didn't have the right to disappear, to die, to abandon them as you and Mama had done.

I was simply going to take a distance in order to diminish my sorrow. I was going to keep on walking, walking, without ever stopping, without ever turning back. My life was no longer going to be a matter of active wandering. Everything continues still. Everything keeps starting over.

GLOSSARY

Abbreviations

A	Arabic	F	French	P	Peul (Pulaar)
E	English	M	Malinke	W	Wolof

List of Linguistic References

Diallo, Abdourahmane. *Grammaire descriptive du pular du Fuuta Jaloo*. Frankfurt am Main: Peter Lang, 2000.

Diouf, Jean-Léopold. *Dictionnaire wolof-français et français-wolof*. Paris: Karthala, 2003.

Fal, Arame, Rosine Santos, et Jean Léonce Doneux. *Dictionnaire wolof-français suivi d'un index français-wolof*. Paris: Karthala, 1990.

Leroy, Anne, et Alpha Oumar Kona Balde. *Parlons poular: Peul du Fouta Djalon*. Paris: L'Harmatan, 2002.

Niang, Dr. Mamadou. *Pulaar-English/English-Pulaar*. New York: Hippocrene Books ("Hippocrene Standard Dictionary"), 1997.

Note on Pronunciation of Peul and Wolof Words

All English/French equivalents are approximate.

I. Vowels

Double vowels are lengthened in pronunciation.

a, à	close to "a" in "father," French /a/; *ñamakaala*
aw	as in "bough"; *taatu-lawbe*
e	"e" in "get," French /ɛ/: *ceeb*
é (W)	as in "wait," but without diphthong, French /e/: *yéet*
ë (W)	as in "better," (2nd "e"), French /ə/: *borom-kër*
i	as in "feet," no diphthong, French /i/: *bilakoro*
o	as in "bought," French /ɔ/: *boowe*
u (W)	as in "you," French /u/: *njulli*
u (P)	as un "put": *njuddu*

GLOSSARY

II. Consonants

Only exceptional consonants are noted; others are similar to English or French.

b (final)	like a "p": *ceeb*
ɓ (P)	an implosive (aspirated) "b": *ɓe*
c (W)	as in "chip": *ceeb, ciip ciip*
ɗ (P)	an implosive" (aspirated) "d": *ñeduɗe*
j	as in "junior": *gejj* (W), *jaaraama* (P)
mb	the "m" is pronounced before the following consonant as in *mbubb* (*boubou*).
nd, ng, nj	the "n" is pronounced before the following consonant, *njulli* (W), *ndjuddu* (P)
ñ	as in "ca*ny*on"

List of Peul and Wolof Terms

alluwal (P)	wooden plank, used as a slate
barki (P)	benediction
baylo (P)	blacksmith
bilakoro (M)	uncircumcised man; a man excluded from the community
bolde (W)	knobbed staff
borom-kër (W)	master, owner of the house
boubou (W)	a large, flowing robe
boowe (P)	grasslands, meadows
ceeb (W)	rice; *ceebu jén* is "rice with fish"
"ciip ciip" (W)	an affected girl (onomatopoetic = bird call)
concession (F)	group of huts for a Muslim family
dibe (P)	earrings
fonde (W)	millet porridge
gaillarde (F)	wench
gejj (W)	dried fish
griotte(s) (F)	the *griotte* (male: *griot*) is a member of the "caste" of poets and musicians who have the role of keeping and relating or performing oral traditions and history of certain West African peoples; this role often includes praise of illustrious or well-known families (the traditional caste system is much criticized as a colonial hierarchical system of exclusion)
hiirde (P)	an evening gathering of song, dance, and story telling

jaaraama (P)	Hello!/Thanks!
kaña (W)	a large rat
kanari (?)	earthen jug
karamoko (P)	master, marabout; Karamoko, used as a name in *The Little Peul*
làmb (W)	hand-to-hand fight, fight arena
leppi (W)	pagne
leymadi (P)	veranda, porch
luumo (P)	fair, weekly market
ñamakaala (P)	"troubadours," itinerant artists
ñàmbi (W)	manioc
N'diago (W)	ethnic group of Casamance
Ndiadiane (Ndiaye)	a legendary Wolof (Serrère) king, legendary founder of the Wolof Kingdom
ndjudu (P)	children born of Peul parents in Senegal; the reference is to *ndjudu dieri*, Guineans born outside of their village, as opposed to *ndjudu walo*, those born within the village
ñedude (P; plur.)	bowls
ngemb (W)	cache-sexe
njulli (W)	a newly circumcised person
pati (P)	grandmother; Paty is the name of the little Peul's grandmother
porto (P)	white, inventor
portocaisse (W)	person from Cap Verd (Cape Verde, Senegal)
sabar (W)	dance, drum
sumbara (P, W)	spice made from the *nere* (fruit from a tree of the mimosa family)
taalibe (W)	pupil of a coranic master
taatu-lawbe (W)	the woodcutter's buttocks (dance)
tabalde (P)	big drum
tubaab (W)	a white person
wàlliyu (W)	a learned, holy person
yéet (W)	an edible gastropod (family, Volutes)

AFTERWORD

To Be Born a Woman   IRÈNE ASSIBA D'ALMEIDA

Often what strikes us most powerfully when we read a work in translation, a work translated from a culture very different than our own, is not the strangeness of what we read but how much it seems familiar. As an adolescent living in Benin, West Africa, I remember reading with delight Mark Twain's *The Adventures of Tom Sawyer,* Charles Dickens's *David Copperfield,* Alain-Fournier's *Le Grand Meaulnes,* and *Anne Frank's Diary.* Difference is there, certainly, but also a recognition of some things we feel we understand, in terms of a motivation or an emotion, of a relationship, of a triumph or a loss. Nothing is exactly the same as in our own world, yet we are made aware of how much all human worlds overlap. This is surely why we want to translate literature from foreign languages and why we read those translations—to enter into the variety of human life and also the commonality of human experience.

For American audiences, Mariama Barry's *The Little Peul* will offer this entry to a world where strangeness and familiarity coexist. Familiarity begins with its subject, one of the most traditional of subjects for a novel, a child's coming of age. The child's development within the family (the very source of "familiarity") and the child's discovery of the constraints of the public world are the subject matter of *The Little Peul.* What is also immediately recognizable to any reader is the clash between those private and public worlds. The mores of the family, the expectations about relationships and roles within the home or through the circuit of blood ties in an extended family, do not always fit with public values in a national (or even international) society. "Globalization," understood as the pressure of new modes of economic and political organization on traditional cultures, has been working its effects for centuries, and in the past century hardly any area, any nation, has been free of those effects. In Barry's novel such economic and political pressures are mainly implicit, and the narrative is not developed as a struggle between diverging economic systems or cultural values. At the same time, however, a reader might see in the domestic arguments between the Little Peul's mother and father a subtle representation of that struggle, but framed in terms of the class and gender preoccupations of their own culture.

The strangeness for a Western reader comes here then, in the circumstances of the child's life and the novel's immersion in the world of the Peul people. Writing in French, Barry is yet able to create a literary version of her world, partly by incorporating examples of the rich Peul tradition—folk stories, legends, proverbs, words in Pulaar—and partly through her depiction of the child's gradual understanding of how that world works, of its economic rules, of the power of relationships between family members, of her restrictions as a child, and particularly as a girl child. The opening scene of the book, which shocked some French reviewers when the novel was originally published, establishes the Little Peul's place in her world, a place that her mother will later try, unsuccessfully, to justify to the girl. Similarly, the Little Peul will confront her father's belief about the economics of earning a living and his ideas of her duties and obligations as his daughter. In each case the girl discovers a gap between her reaction to the situation at hand and what she has been taught her reaction should be. She will also see an even greater discrepancy, and a more emotionally potent one, as she observes her parents' actions contradicting their words. That contradiction, which appears to the child as a lie and a betrayal, in turn gives confidence to her own judgments. Barry's novel tells the important story of the development of a child into a cultural dissenter, a story familiar but unfamiliar, original in the context of the Little Peul's world.

Mariama Barry was born in Dakar, Senegal, but was raised partly in her parent's homeland, Guinea. Her family's ethnic origins were among the Peul, a pastoral, nomadic people, first given historical mention in the tenth century, who moved across the African continent from Senegal to Sudan. Converted to Islam in the 1700s, the Peul founded a number of Muslim kingdoms, one of which, the Fuuta Jaloo, was centered in what is now the national territory of Guinea. In 1958 this nation was the first to obtain independence in Francophone West Africa, though it would retain French as the official language of government. As in the rest of West Africa, French had also become an important literary language—even if often a contested one—and in the 1950s Guinea produced two works in French now considered classics of African literature, Camara Laye's autobiography, *L'enfant noir* (*The Dark Child*) (1953), and Djibril Tamsir Niane's *Soundjata ou l'épopée Mandingue* (*Sundiata, an Epic of Old Mali*) (1960).

Though Mariama Barry's *The Little Peul* has a subject similar to Camara Laye's early autobiography, in the fifty years spread between the two works a great deal changed in Africa and in African literature. Without doubt the single most significant change in that literature has been the emergence of women writers throughout Francophone Africa. Modern African literature in European languages took shape as a corpus in the 1930s, yet it was not until the mid-1960s that Francophone African women began to appear in print, while their work only began to be seen as a corpus in the 1980s. Despite starting late by several decades, the women who began to write initiated a widespread movement that has continued to expand and grow, a "prise d'écriture," a "seizing of writing," a "right to write"—as it were—from a deeply patriarchal society in which women would not be writers. Women began using this new writing—this powerful medium—to represent themselves in a femino-centric perspective, to portray themselves as actors instead of spectators and place themselves at the core instead of the periphery of a new literature.

With this new power of the pen (and the typewriter and the computer) women have explored, deplored, subverted, and sought to redress the status quo within their fiction. If the inscription of a more "authentic" gendered-self was at the heart of their preoccupations, that work had to be done through a kind of subversion, though at the time they began, the mere act of writing was, for a woman, an act of subversion. This subversive undercurrent appeared in their choice of themes and how they treated those themes. The issues running through their fiction were important especially to women: the culture of compulsory motherhood, the demand that they produce male children, questions about abortion, excision, and prostitution, and, always, the plight of children. It was equally important, however, that they created women who celebrated the community of women, the joys of friendship, the importance of love, the beauty of the female body not as a site of abuse but of pleasure. And, of course, the introduction of these matters into their fiction did not mean they neglected other stories and ideas. Addressing themselves to the continent's many forms of social and political life, women writers have produced some of the most trenchant and severe assessments of African politics, philosophies, and morals. They have been, and continue to be, *engagées*, committed to the whole of their culture and for the betterment of their society.

Women's writing in Francophone Africa is still a relatively new art, continuing to produce original and surprising young writers, who are building on the still recent work of their immediate predecessors and models. Mariama Barry has thus benefitted from the foundations laid by novelists of the 1980s and 1990s (many of them, of course, still active writers), and her vital connection to their work is evident. In the matter of form, for instance, the autobiography has been a favored genre for African women, while in an interview Barry described *The Little Peul* as "une biographie romanesque" (a fictional biography), and whether or not the novel's events match the author's life, its narrative clearly has the form of an autobiography. It is possible to see a brief "tradition" for the form of autobiography even among writing emerging specifically from the Peul culture, in Kesso Barry's *Kesso, Princesse peuhle* (Kesso, a Peul princess)(1988) and Amadou Hampaté Bâ's *Amkoullel,*

AFTERWORD

l'enfant peul (Amkoullel, the Peul child) (1991). Still, the more profound influence on *The Little Peul* is not in the choice of genre but the subject matter: the ideas about the position of women in society, the questions of cultural authority/identity, the realistic view of conflicts within the family around gender relations, these are the important topics that Barry draws into her fiction and addresses in her own way.

To say that the subject of Barry's novel is a child's coming of age hardly does justice to the story's twists and turns, its elaboration, advances, and withdrawals. Written as a series of un-numbered "chapters," from one paragraph to several pages in length, the story follows the Little Peul from early childhood through her first years in the Koranic and French schools until, on the verge of adolescence, she comes to live in her grand-mother's home, in a village close to Labé, the capital of the Fuuta Jaloo. In Barry's writing the style is simple but engaging, and the effect of this style is not impressionistic but accumula-tive—as a human personality develops as a result of experience on whatever is intrinsic in the person. The growth of the girl's character follows from the events strung along Barry's narra-tive thread.

Barry establishes this pattern with great power by opening her novel on a scene of female excision. She describes how the Little Peul and a group of other girls, six or seven years of age, are forcibly excised, a scene that unforgettably etches on the reader's mind the cultural subjection of the female body. It is an initiation, fictively for the reader and literally for the Little Peul, into what it is expected of a woman in Peul society. It would be mistaken, however, to say on the basis of the book's first chapter that this is a novel about excision, or even pri-marily about the oppression of the female body. Barry herself deplored the attention, bordering on sensation, given the exci-sion scene when the novel was first published, and in a later interview remarked: "It is a shame that all the other aspects of the book have been erased. People speak only of excision. They only have eyes for excision, especially in Europe." To a degree critics have followed the lead of journalists and made the excision a focal point of their discussions of the novel, so *The Little Peul* is now linked with novels such as Fatou Keita's *Rebelle* (1998), a novel that does deal primarily with excision, or with Barry's *Kesso, princesse peuhle,* which also includes an excision scene.

What Barry objected to was the assumption that excision should be seen as the primary event in the girl's life, when in the novel it is only the first example of the series of encounters with tradition and the expectations of others that will create a rebel. Though it is extremely traumatic, the most important part of the scene is not excision itself, but the girl's reaction to the mutilation of her body, the beginning of the growth of self-awareness and her ability to critique, and eventually to resist, the pattern of "pre-ordained" events meant to direct a woman's life in African/Peul society:

> The week you were born [her mother says], I pierced your ears with a needle and thread so they would not become infected. . . . That was your first initiation. The second was placing you in the coranic school so you could turn toward your Creator, learn to do your ablutions, your prayers, and recite the Qur'an properly. As for what just took place, it has made you grow because you had not yet experienced suffering. You were a child who knew only joy and had no cares. Because this trial was painful, it has brought you a new power, that of overcoming suffering. And when you are older, your menstruation will begin. That will give you access to the world of women. On your wedding night, as soon as your husband has taken your virginity, you will be an adult woman. And as a woman, when you have your first child, you will crouch with your teeth biting into a rag or a piece of wood, because you must not cry out. And, with your first child, you will finally be like me. You will have experienced all that I have experienced, and in the same order. (13)

This is the path that a woman is predestined to tread, and it is given to the Little Peul from her mother, who herself received it from her own mother. What is interesting here is that although the Little Peul does not totally understand what has happened to her through the excision, she understands enough to decide: "I already knew that I would not pass on this traumatizing experience. And in fact, I was to fight much later to be the only sacrificial victim within and beyond my family" (15). Thus from an early age, the Little Peul desires to break the chain of women's suffering. She grows more intent in her resolve as she sees the double standards that prevail in her society in relation to gender. Although her father encourages her to go to school—though he does not always give her the means to do so—most girls around her are prevented from attending school because they "had to remain home to learn how to 'care for and keep' their future husband" (26) or for fear that they would become too smart—and so a threat to "male supremacy."

When the mother leaves the household, the girl is expected to assume her work, at age twelve no less, taking care of the home and cooking for everybody. Her brothers now refuse to help since, having gone through circumcision, they have become men and must be served by women. At this point the Little Peul suddenly revolts. She hits on the idea of a domestic strike, refusing to cook for the family. In three days they are begging her to resume the cooking, her brothers magically agreeing to help her. When she discovers the power of the kitchen, her only regret is that the idea of a strike had not occurred to her earlier. She also seems to recognize her mother's connection to her actions, saying "I must have dissidence in my genes" (111).

However, if the Little Peul learned from the mother's example, the mother herself still has mixed feelings about her position as a woman. She will seek a divorce—forbidden to her within traditional Peul culture, but she eventually manages to get it through the means of modern law. She is independent, works to be self-reliant, and insists on education for her daughter as means of being self-sufficient too: "You have to succeed. A good diploma and a good job, these are the real husband for a woman, do you understand?" (130). Yet, she also conceives of success within the traditional norms of marriage and child bearing, saying: "I would have liked to give you a different image of myself rather than that of a woman living outside of marriage" (129). She critiques the Peul institutions and mores, while expressing a veiled regret that she lives outside their norms: "Society condemns me because I am not in the institution of marriage in which one is supposed to live and die even when you don't like it. My family tells me that I am dragging their name through mud and shame. So I've lost you, my children, when you are my only success" (130). If the mother's words send mixed signals, the mother's actions proclaim her a rebel.

If there is a single theme, or extended situation, that provides the primary narrative impetus for the novel, it is the conflict between the girl's parents, which divides their home and finally leads to the mother's departure and their divorce. To quote Barry's interview again, "This book is filled with the pain of my parents' divorce" (see note 1). The Little Peul often expresses this pain as an alienation and an increasingly critical distance from her parent's demands. Her relationship with her father apparently includes love, affection, and understanding. In contrast, that with her mother is difficult, characterized by tension, by violence, by her mother's unwillingness to show any love for her daughter. Yet neither parent, with their opposite approaches, seems able to understand the child's intimate confusions, or the cultural basis of her resistance to them. Though both are of Guinea and of Peul backgrounds, the father and mother are significantly different in their class origins, and this difference gives them very dissimilar values and aspirations for their lives. Barry's realism sees beyond the emotional relations within family life and looks closely at the economic motivations of actions. She understands that family dynamics are not only a matter of love, and the Little Peul, though only a child, assimilates and comes to understand her parent's diverging points of view in regards to money matters and economic success.

In the course of the novel not only will the mother and father split apart over financial disagreements, but each of them will also attempt to take economic advantage of their daughter, by taking money she has earned herself or by exploiting her labor. How can the child make sense of their demands, or fit their actions into any set of values they teach? One of the strengths of Barry's novel is to make all of the characters' actions understandable, even if they are also depicted as hypocritical or cruel. These contradictions suggest again the commonality underlying difference, the problems common everywhere, and thus Adam Philip's remark on a Western view of relations between child and parent seems also relevant to Mariama Barry's world: "Children unavoidably treat their parents as though they were experts on life. They, and other adults, are the people from whom the child learns what is necessary. But the extent to which children make demands on adults which the adults don't know what to do with is not sufficiently remarked on." For the Little Peul, as for children everywhere, "what is necessary" must be discovered by an often painful matching of words against actions, of setting what's expected against what they discover is in fact unnecessary, or even impossible.

The Little Peul's experience of her parents' conflicting attitudes and values help her to realize her independence. But she is not without a more useful model in her life, the grandmother with whom she is living at the novel's close. The grandmother, who exudes magnificent serenity before old age and death, teaches her granddaughter about love, beauty, the importance of work, the value of speech and of silence. The grandmother deliberately pretends to be hard of hearing, even deaf, in order to "hear" only what she pleases. She nourishes the Little Peul with the wisdom of her age and leads her toward understanding some of the difficult questions of life: "our dead" she says "are not dead—they are among us somewhere; they see us, but we cannot see them" (158). She also tries to make the child see that "growing old isn't a burden, but a privilege" (159), and reminds her that a full stomach may summon the spirit, but the spirit then "loses its awareness of the most important things in life" (170). Her aunt also has some advice to give her niece: "Stop judging and especially comparing—just observe.

Be sparing of words and develop your sense of observation—you'll need it more than your mouth" (147), or again: "You have to learn to walk on people's wounds without hurting them" (152). Good advice to understand what is happening to those around you and then to be able to get along with them. The Little Peul's strong character is shaped by the very strong women who surround her—mother, grandmother, aunt—who each in their own way find strategies of avoidance, of dissent, in a word, of survival, to respond to the demands that patriarchy imposes on women in Peul society.

Notes

1. Interview with Mariama Barry by Sentinelle, www.seneweb.com/news/engine/print_article.php?artid=15060; my translation.
2. Adam Philip, "The Experts," *London Review of Books*, December 22, 1994, p. 24.